Multiplication

By

Tommy Barnett

Creation

Printed in the United States of America
Library of Congress Catalog Card Number: 96-71395
International Standard Book Number: 0-88419-450-7

Creation House
Strang Communications Company
600 Rinehart Road
Lake Mary, FL 32746
Phone: 407-333-3132
Fax: 407-333-7100
Web site: http://www.creationhouse.com

Unless otherwise noted, all Scripture quotations are from the King James Version of the Bible.

Contents

MULTIPLICATION

CONTENTS

INTRODUCTION

God's Multiplication Factors

At the beginning of 1996, I stood before Phoenix First Assembly and preached my New Year's message. I paraphrased a D.L. Moody thought by saying, "Revival is not anything mysterious. Revival comes in response to the amount of prayer we pray."

I challenged our people to do four things in the following month:

1. To pray every day for the next month.
2. To fast one day a week, asking God to send a great revival to our church.
3. To bring an unsaved person with them every Sunday morning for a month.
4. To tithe for a month.

Ninety percent of the congregation stood up to indicate they would make this commitment. One thousand people promised to host prayer groups in their home that month. Some women began coming to the church to pray all night. Others stayed for an entire week, praying around the clock, taking breaks only to sleep and shower.

What happened after that month was awesome. Scores of people were saved, and our people brought them to the church immediately. We kept a pastor in the church twenty-four hours a day to receive their public confessions and baptize them. Revival exploded in our midst.

A fresh, powerful anointing fell on me and upon the church. At every service hundreds of people would come to get saved. More than 30,000 people stood to accept Christ as their Savior during the week of our Easter Pageant, and more than 150,000 people attended the services. All this happened while we were praying. God was multiplying our growth.

> Then had the churches rest throughout all Judea and Galilee and Samaria, and were edified; and walking in the fear of the Lord, and in the comfort of the Holy Ghost, and multiplied (Acts 9:31).

People began to give money for our ministries which were growing at the rapid pace of multiplication. At the same time that revival was sweeping our church, a man who did not even attend our church approached me about giving money for a retirement village. There were eleven acres to the north of the church that we had always wanted to buy and use for a retirement village. We had offered $2 million ten years earlier, but the owners wouldn't sell. Miraculously, they offered to sell it to us for $700,000 less than the previous offer.

That was a wonderful reduction, but we did not have that kind of money. I met with an Assembly of God brother who is extremely well-known for building retirement villages. After doing a study on the need for such a venture, he made arrangements to buy the land and to work with us to minister there to the elderly. As a result of prayer, that eleven acres will be one of the most wonderful retirement villages in the country.

A layman from our church who was a professional football player and started our Athletes in Ministry (AIM), Larry Kerychuk, become world-known for his ministry to athletes. This wonderful ministry has touched many people, including Coach Bill McCartney of Promise Keepers; David Robinson, an all-pro basketball all-star; and Evander Holyfield, the heavyweight boxing champion of the world.

Larry was directed by God to build an Olympic training site where world-class athletes can train physically and spiritually for a year. As we prayed, and revival grew in our church, a man who does not even attend our church came forward with a gift of $5 million dollars to pay for the facility. It will have an olympic-sized pool, a soccer field, athletic courts, track and field facilities and weight rooms. Another man, not a member of our church, wanted to build an inner-city gymnasium and enlisted the help of world-renowned architect Jack DeBartello. After visiting our ministry in Los Angeles, this same man not only got saved, but also gave $1.5 million dollars to build an inner-city gymnasium for our Church on the Street. Our Master's Commission had prayed for this gym for years.

The Los Angeles International Church has experienced multiplication as well, growing to reach more than twenty thousand people each month in over one hundred ministries. I had always believed that someone in my lifetime would give me a million dollars to help finance the ministry. During this prayer revival, a man gave me a million dollars. Another man gave a million dollars to help pay off the building in Los Angeles. Multiplication was happening with people and with resources.

Throughout this book, I will share with you about these ministries and how God multiplied both people and resources. Multiplication started when we committed ourselves to prayer and seeking God. But the glory belongs to the Lord. Prepare yourself to read stories and discover life-giving factors about how God multiplies His church.

God Multiplies People For His Work

God cares about people — not about buildings, programs, methods or styles. God cares about you and me so much that He sent His Son to show us His love and die for us. Now that's love.

I pray daily that the Lord of the harvest will send workers — you and me — to reap a harvest of souls. My prayer is that all of us become soul-winners. The vision God has given me is threefold: to build a great church as a pattern of good works; to share with and challenge pastors how to build great churches; and to write books to help others grow great churches.

It has been my privilege to see our church in Phoenix grow into one of the largest churches in the nation. My excitement is not that we are so big, but that God is doing such big things through us — saving thousands of souls. I am consumed with seeing the lost saved, and I desire for that same soul-winning fire to wax hot within you.

I want you to get to know something about me. God has really done a wonderful work in me through the power of the Holy Spirit. You see, if God can save and use me, a shy, midwestern boy, He can do mighty things in your life as well.

MULTIPLICATION

Small Beginnings, Big Dreams

Dust and tumbleweed blow through the small West Texas town of Electra, home to less than seven thousand country folks. My birth in a little, yellow frame house brought an interesting comment from the doctor. He said that there was a veil over my face at birth. Old-timers tell me that a child born with a veil-covered face would be used of God in a special way.

Dad was a traveling evangelist who would sit me on a pulpit and teach me to memorize and recite scripture. He would say, "Go...," and I would be expected to reply, "...into all the world and preach the gospel to every creature." I have never forgotten that verse. The lost that need to be saved are the major focus of my ministry, and joy fills me whenever someone receives Jesus.

God was at work in my life. When I was thirteen years old, I announced in our church that God had called me to preach. My parents were very supportive of my call to preach the gospel. One day I went to Dad and said, "Dad, I feel that it is time I start out."

"Son," he said, "let's just pray about it. If it is God's will God will work it out.

"We have been praying about it since I was thirteen; it is time we do something about it," I replied.

"OK, son," he said, "we won't tell anybody you want to preach, but if someone asks you to hold a revival then we will know that it is God's will for you to preach."

"Good deal," I answered. I didn't know that people rarely go around asking short, sawed-off runts like myself to preach a revival.

God's Anointing to Preach My First Revival

My dad went down to visit his mother, who was near death. As he prepared to return home, waving good-bye to the family, my uncle, a missionary-turned-pastor, said, "Why don't you ask Tommy to come and hold a revival for me?"

My dad almost fainted. "How did you know he wanted to preach?" he asked.

"I didn't know," my uncle replied. "But I just felt as if I should say that."

My dad rushed home to tell me. He helped me buy an organ to take with me and an old, gray Jeep station wagon. A fifteen-year-old friend was going with me to play the organ.

I arrived at a little, west Texas church in Seminole, Texas. There were about seventy people in attendance. I had never preached a revival, so I got on my knees and prayed, "Oh God, I don't want to preach because my dad was a preacher. I don't want to preach because my uncle and aunts are preachers. I don't want to do it because of tradition or because it is expected. O God, it has to be You. Father, I pray that You will save at least fifty people in this revival if it is Your will for me to preach. And fill twenty-five people with the Holy Spirit."

Even as a young man, I was certain of three things: *purpose, people* and *prayer.* I knew God's purpose in my preaching was to save people. And I knew the only way for that to happen was through prayer. I also wanted to know for certain that His purpose for my life was to preach.

What I didn't know was how hard it would be to get

people saved. If I had known how difficult it is to get people to respond to a salvation message, then I would have prayed, "Lord, if it be your will save two and fill one with the Holy Spirit." I did ask, "O God, you have got to fill me with your Spirit. God, fill me with a fresh anointing."

The afternoon before the first time I would speak, the Spirit of God came upon me. I stood up not as a sixteen-year-old weakling boy. I stood up as a man filled with the Holy Spirit. I preached on the verse, "What should it profit a man if he gain the whole world and lose his soul?" Seven people walked to the altar. From that day forward, I felt God's anointing.

More opportunities to preach presented themselves. I began to travel around the world and preach the gospel at outdoor soccer meetings and revival meetings. The day came when God put it in my heart to pastor a church. I sent my name to all the big churches, but none of them even wrote me back. I thought the world was just waiting for this evangelist to come and pastor, but I found out that many churches believe evangelists do not make good pastors. So I sent my name out to the medium-sized churches, but they did not write back either. Then I sent my name to the small churches, and not even a small church replied.

So I decided to go back to basics: Pray! I know I should have prayed in the first place. God's grace is abundant, and I prayed, "God, no matter what church you open, I will take it."

I received a phone call from a deacon in a church in Davenport, Iowa. He said, "Pastor, would you consider coming to preach? We'd like you to consider taking our church. Would you pray about it?"

"Would I?" I replied. "I have already prayed about it. It is God's will."

I went to meet with the deacon board. I wasn't impressed. They had had six pastors in ten years. The last one, younger than I, had a heart attack and almost died. The total income of the church was twenty thousand dollars a year, including the pastor's salary. You might say they couldn't get a *good* pastor, so they hired me.

Experiencing God's Anointing in Davenport

The first Sunday morning that I preached, nobody was saved. I went home and prayed all afternoon. I felt the Spirit of God and His anointing on my life. That night four people accepted Jesus. God's consuming fire began to burn in me, and my preaching became bold and fearless. I really had not known how to build a church. I knew how to win souls but not how to equip and mature the saints. God was beginning to teach me the multiplication factors that would equip a church to grow in numbers and mature in Christ at the same time. Our church grew from seventy-six people to over four thousand members in eight years.

I was fearless even in the face of confrontations with the forces of the enemy. The critical media blistered me; some of our youth were arrested and thrown into jail for handing out tracts in front of pornographic book stores and massage parlors; we faced a long court fight and threats were made against our church. Threats were even made against me and my family. The porno shop owners threatened to molest and brutally attack my wife, mailing filthy pictures to her depicting what they would do to her when I was out of town.

One day some enemies tracked her down in a car and pulled her over. She jumped out and ran to a nearby house, flung the door open and went inside. The attacker ran back to his car. The lady in the house was scared to death and asked, "How did you get in?"

"I came in the front door," my wife told her.

"No, you didn't," she replied. "I just bolted the door and put a chain on it. It has three locks. There is no way you got in through that door." Now I am not spooky, but I believe God supernaturally protected my wife.

God did wonderful things in the city. But a time came when the fire went out within my soul. I sat down and wrote out my resignation for the church. Then one night I was in my office praying at about midnight. No one except Marja knew I was there. Suddenly the back door opened, and old Brother Shotwell, a retired minister, walked into my office and asked, "Pastor, what are you doing here?" I told him what had happened to me, and he said, "What you need is fresh oil." The old man put his hands on my head and anointed me. I felt as though someone had just opened up the oil of God's anointing and poured it all over me.

There are times when we all need fresh oil. That is one reason I have written this book. I am praying that God will use this book to pour fresh oil on, and light a new fire in, you. Churches need fresh oil; individuals need fresh oil. Bible schools need fresh oil. Bus drivers need fresh oil. Elders, deacons and deaconesses need fresh oil. Choir members and staff members need fresh oil. We all need fresh oil. As our Christian lives unfold, our ministries increase and our responsibilities grow, we need fresh oil and fire in our lives.

Moved by God to Phoenix

I loved our church in Davenport. I had planned to stay there until I died. I had a beautiful little home on four acres outside of town. It was on the side of a hill with a beautiful creek running through it.

Though I had no plans to move, I woke up one morning without the conscious presence of God. I have noticed that when God wants to get my attention, He withdraws His presence. I would rather die than to lose an intimate awareness of God's presence.

It was during that time I received a call to come to Phoenix, Arizona. I had been in Phoenix one time in the middle of summer as the speaker at a church growth conference. I had decided right then that I never wanted to go to Phoenix. The heat was stifling.

I determined to go and just fulfill my obligation and then return home to Iowa. But God spoke to me, "I want you to leave your child. I will give you, as I did Abraham, one hundredfold of what I gave you in Davenport, Iowa." That's 200,000! How could that come to pass?

But I went back to Iowa, and with tears streaming down my cheeks, I told the people that I was going to have to resign to go to Phoenix. As I drove out of the city, I wept for many miles.

I did not think that I could love another church. I wondered if God would ever move again. On the first Sunday in Phoenix I walked onto the platform and sat down, tired and unmotivated. The choir sang, "It is going to be a great day." When they hit the last note it was as if the windows of heaven were opened. I was conscious of the presence of God again. There was a fresh anointing in my life.

MULTIPLICATION

Our church began to grow, so we sold our building and built a new one. I will never forget the morning that our new building with its 6,500-seat auditorium was finished. We had prayed for this building. We had fasted for the money to pay for it. At last it was done, and suddenly fear hit me. *You don't have enough people to fill this big building,* I thought. *Aren't you going to be embarrassed when only a few hundred people show up?*

All week long before the first service I had prayed, "Oh God, give us some people. Don't let me be embarrassed." Before we started, I peaked out the door to see if anybody had come. The building was not only filled, there were people sitting in the aisles. Then I really got scared. That is the way we are at times. We pray that God will answer our prayer, and then it scares us to death when He does.

I ran back to my office and fell on my knees. "God, what am I going to do? I am not a big preacher. I am just a country preacher that has never been to the country. I can't go out there. I wasn't made to pastor a big church like this. I am not a big man. God, you have done this miracle."

Someone knocked on the door and said, "They are getting ready to start."

I said, "God, I am not going to go out there unless you fill me with fresh oil." Suddenly I felt it run over the top of my head, down upon my chest and into that cavity inside that was made only for God. It went down to my loins and down my thighs to my feet. I stood up, put my Bible under my arm with all the confidence of Daniel as he marched into the lions' den, and walked onto the platform.

The Lord stopped me from preaching the sermon I had prepared. I opened my Bible and preached on the subject, "The Glory Belongs to Him Alone." I said, "Let the buses be blown up if they take away from the glory of God [that took the grace of God for me to talk about buses that way]. Let the choir be dismantled if it takes away from the glory of God. Let the building be destroyed, and let us meet out in the open if we give it any of God's glory. Let the man behind the pulpit be cut down if he takes any of the glory. God, and He alone, is altogether lovely."

God has blessed us because we have always lifted up Jesus. If anything, we play down the role of the leadership. We know that God uses people to lead, but we also know that as long as we remain little in our own eyes, giving Him all the glory, we will always have the blessings of God.

Reaching Out for Christ in Los Angeles

There is one more anointing I want to share with you. God placed not a burden but a call in my heart for Los Angeles. A burden comes and goes, but a call remains steadfast.

God called us to minister in Los Angeles. The call was birthed in our hearts three years before we responded. We started, and God blessed, but it seemed as if there were a heaviness over the city. I believe there is an oppression over that city, forces in operation that affect people physically and spiritually.

A battle raged in my soul. One night I called my son, Matthew, who co-pastors the Los Angeles International Church and heads up the ministry at the Dream Center in Los Angeles. "Matthew, we have to pray this thing through," I said to him. "I am going to get on a plane after our Sunday night service and fly there. We are going to pray all night long. If you want to gather a few together, that's OK."

Ninety people stayed to pray through the night. In prayer, we sought God's purpose as His people. We prayed, "Oh God, break the bondage in this city."

Alone, I prayed, "Oh God, I need a fresh anointing for this city. You gave me one for Phoenix. I will be honest, God, I have a burden for Phoenix, but I don't have a burden — just a call — for Los Angeles. Give me a burden. God, give me a love for these people. I just don't have that love like I should for them. Anoint me with fresh oil."

Again it happened. The fire ignited and fresh oil poured over me. The chains were broken. About four o'clock in the morning we walked around the Los Angeles International Church, located on one of the most dangerous city blocks in Los Angeles.

We got so excited that I said, "Let's go around again!" We went around again; then I said, "I'll tell you what we are going to do. We are going to ask God to empty the sixteen houses located around the church so that we can fill them with people who get saved in our church. If we put twenty persons in a house, that's three hundred and fifty people we can win to the Lord. We'll put them into those houses, disciple them, bring them out of bondage and help them to be set free." We marched and agreed in prayer.

As we prayed, God revealed His purpose to His people, and a fresh anointing fell in that service. Today God is multiplying disciples through the ministry in Los Angeles. Over 130 ministries are in full force, and hundreds are being saved and set free.

Your ministry or your Christian walk may need fresh oil and fire. As you read this book, God wants to ignite you so that through you He can multiply disciples for His kingdom. I pray that His purpose will be revealed to you through prayer so that many people around you will be saved and discipled in Jesus Christ.

Remember, God has a purpose and a plan for His people. Throughout history, He has acted in love to build saving relationships with people. God's purpose for people is simple: to have an eternal, loving relationship with Him by faith in His Son, Jesus Christ. To implement God's purpose, pray and obey His command to go into all the world to share the good news about salvation in Christ Jesus.

The only way the good news of Jesus Christ spreads throughout the earth is through people. People loving, witnessing, caring, nurturing and sharing become Christ's ambassadors on every street and in every neighborhood, town and city. People are important to God!

God's desire is for people to be saved through faith in Jesus Christ. Church buildings, programs, methods and the like are important in their place. But their place is never more important than people. The church exists to bring people to a saving knowledge of Jesus Christ.

As Jesus ascended into heaven, He left us with a command, not a suggestion. His command focused on people.

> Go ye therefore, and teach all nations [people], baptizing them in the name of the Father, and of the Son, and of the Holy Ghost: teaching them to observe all things whatsoever I have commanded you: and, lo, I am with you always, even unto the end of the world (Matt. 28:19-20).

MULTIPLICATION

Jesus framed His command with this emphasis: "But ye shall receive power, after that the Holy Ghost is come upon you; and ye shall be witnesses unto me both in Jerusalem, and in all Judea, and in Samaria, and unto the uttermost part of the earth" (Acts 1:8). In other words, we are given Holy Spirit power to witness everywhere on earth to people.

We often comment that the book of Acts is about the acts of the Holy Spirit. But what is the purpose for the Holy Spirit's actions? The Holy Spirit acts in and through people so that people will be saved, healed, delivered and restored. The Holy Spirit does much more than add people to the church!

Follow this closely. In Acts 4:4 we read the report that "many of them which heard the word believed; and the number of the men was about five thousand."

Now the numbers of people being saved continued to increase in the early church. Those saved were so numerous that they were no longer called a crowd but rather a multitude (Acts 4:32). The Holy Spirit added more and more to this multitude of believers (Acts 5:14).

The account in Acts 6 indicates that something very wonderful had begun to happen. Up until this time the church grew by addition. People were *added* to the church daily. One brings one to Christ. Two lead two to salvation. That is certainly wonderful growth in the body of Christ. But God desires more than addition in the church.

Multiplication is God's way to produce exponential growth. Multiplication superceded addition in Acts 6:1,7:

> In those days, when the number of disciples *multiplied*...the word of God increased, and the

> number of disciples *multiplied* in Jerusalem greatly; and a great company of the priests were obedient to the faith" (italics added).

With addition, four plus four is eight. But with multiplication, four times four is sixteen. The church began to grow by multiplication — not just addition.

Let me give you a simple illustration of the difference between multiplication and addition. Suppose that I gave you a choice between a one-thousand-dollar gift on the first day of January or a one-penny gift on the first day of January which doubled every day in the month. Which would you choose? For your sake, I hope you choose the penny. After the first week your choice might not look so great — you would have two pennies on the second day, four on the third day, eight on the fourth day, sixteen on day five, thirty-two on day six and only sixty-four pennies by day seven. But if you kept multiplying each day's total by two, at the end of the month that penny would have grown to over $21 million dollars! That is exponential growth through multiplication. The early church multiplied, and that's God's desire for us today.

In this book, I will explore these questions with you:

- What causes exponential growth in the life of the church?
- How do we move in the Spirit from addition to multiplication? What factors are involved?
- How can we learn from Scripture what is essential for multiplying the numbers of people saved daily?

MULTIPLICATION

I will also share the awesome multiplication results God has produced as He multiplies disciples in the church. I call these miracle stories — Multiplication Results.

Purpose-driven people, filled by the Spirit with visionary dreams and praying for His power, will multiply the church in this generation. The multiplication results are an end-time harvest of exponential proportions for the kingdom of God. I believe the revival now unfolding in America will be a multiplication revival.

Are you ready? As believers, pastors and church leaders, we need to know how to implement the multiplication factors that will bring in a harvest greater than any generation has ever witnessed. Heed the call of Christ because the kingdom of God is right here in our midst (Luke 10:2-3,8-10).

Just in the past few days as I worked on finishing this manuscript, I have observed the following evidences that the church is in *Multiplication*:

- More than 25,000 people attended recent Sunday services in our church.
- On the same Sunday, Matthew had more than 20,000 people attend the Christmas activities in Los Angeles.
- In Dayton, Ohio, my son, Luke, has seen his church grow from two hundred people to an attendance of more than two thousand people for his singing Christmas tree service.
- My former associate pastor, Jack Wallace, who now pastors in Detroit, Michigan, had more than eight thousand attend services on one recent Sunday.
- My former associate, Bill Wilson, who heads up

> Metro Church in New York City, had more than 25,000 people attend services on one Sunday recently, and he gave away more than 20,000 Christmas presents.

I preach at multiple services weekly in Phoenix, travel and speak to churches all over America, minister in Los Angeles, and serve on a multitude of boards while wondering how to multiply my life over and over again. I am experiencing personal multiplication in God's work and seeing multiplication happen wherever I go.

Let me share some multiplication factors with you which are working to reach the end-time harvest that Jesus prophecied in Luke 10:2-3:

> The harvest truly is great, but the laborers are few: pray ye therefore the Lord of the harvest, that he would send forth laborers into his harvest.

FACTOR #1

Multiply by Networking

> Then had the churches rest throughout all Judea and Galilee and Samaria, and were edified; and walking in the fear of the Lord, and in the comfort of the Holy Ghost, were multiplied (Acts 9:31).

In our congregation we find hurts and meet them. In order to do that we must network people and ministries with one another. Handicapped people needed ministry so we developed a wheelchair ministry. Others loved to grow flowers and tend to the grounds, so they developed a ministry to meet that need.

All in all, more than two hundred ministries network together in Phoenix, and more than one hundred and thirty ministries network together in Los Angeles. Let me use the example of the Los Angeles International Church to illustrate how networking leads to multiplication.

When I went to Los Angeles, I noticed that there were many small ministries but that nothing was really flourishing. I didn't know how to reach that city. So I invited many of the existing ministries to house their work at the Dream Center campus — formerly the Queen of Angels Hospital complex. I asked them to help us minister to Los Angeles in return for lodging, food and office space.

One of my former associates from Davenport, who was like a son to me, now has a tremendous sidewalk Sunday school outreach in the Bronx. Bill Wilson networked with us to start a similar ministry in downtown Los Angeles. Now he travels back and forth between New York and Los Angeles, overseeing the Sidewalk Sunday school ministry.

There was a motorcycle church in our area that was having some difficulties, so the pastor asked to come under our ministry covering.

A ministry called Hope for Hollywood had been operating for seventeen years under the leadership of an Assembly of God missionary. He worked with runaway kids that came to the streets of Los Angeles from all over the nation. If they were not rescued in two weeks, the runaways would end up in prostitution and drugs.

"Why don't you join with us?" I asked him. He had never had a place to house the kids, but now he has a home to minister to runaways who have been saved and rescued from the streets.

Another man in the city feeds 150,000 a week. He secures food products from all over the area. Now he feeds the people at the Dream Center, and we minister to their spiritual needs. We are also networking with a ministry out of Nashville that is establishing a home for unwed mothers.

Rick Seaward came to Los Angeles from Singapore. He is bringing forty people that will train and equip indigenous, ethnic pastors to return to their countries and plant churches. Scores of ethnic communities live in the Los Angeles. area — Asians, South Americans, Africans, Arabs and others. These people already understand their own cultures and languages. We will equip them to go back to their own countries and win people to Jesus Christ.

Churches have been established for Filipinos, Cambodians, Koreans, Russians and Armenians as well as Spanish-speaking individuals and Messianic Jews. Multiplication is cross-cultural. The gospel first went from Jews to Samaritans and then into the gentile nations of the world. That same multiplication factor works today in God's church. America's largest cities are now becoming mission fields filled with people from nations all over the globe.

Networking provides the ability to release people while at the same time giving them a covering. That is a dimension of multiplication. You cannot multiply anything if you hold on too tightly.

Our Pastors' Schools in Phoenix and Los Angeles are examples of networking. We have held these schools for over twenty years. The concept started when I realized that I was spending too much time showing individual pastors and church leaders how we lead our church ministries. I said "Let's set a date to bring in pastors from all over, and we'll show them how we minister here." Our Pastors' School was born out of a need, and now it's the largest Pastors' School in the world. In fact, many of the pastors who attend the Pastors' School have helped us with the funding needed to build the Dream Center at Los Angeles International Church (LAIC).

Multiplication will be the last great end-time revival.

We live in the end-times. The harvest is ripe and ready. Amos 9:13 describes our times: "Behold, the days come, saith the Lord, that the plowman shall overtake the reaper, and the treader of grapes him that soweth seed; and the mountains shall drop sweet wine, and all the hills shall melt." In times such as these, we need to stop the competition among churches in a city. Instead of trying to attract one another's sheep, we need to network together to win the lost in our cities to Jesus Christ.

Factor #1
Churches that network will multiply.

Ask yourself:

- Does my church network with other ministries to win our city for Christ?
- Do we give permission to our church members to find needs and meet them?
  What needs should be met right now, and who will meet them?

Pray...

— for the wisdom to seek out and network in ministry with other Christians.

— for your church to find needs and meet them.

— for multiplication to happen through networking ministries.

Factor #2

Live the Vicarious Life

The multiplier multiplies himself by expressing his vision to his leadership. Others catch that vision and multiply. A pastor or church leader must be a person of vision who can express his vision to other leaders.

Articulate the vision. The Christian multiplier...

- lives a vicarious life. Seeing other people reach their dreams gives him as much joy, or more, than reaching his own dream.
- believes in people.
- knows that some will fail and some will succeed.
- is willing to take the losses along with the gain.
- has a vision and articulates that vision to others.
- heals and does not wound people.
- makes God and people his first priority.
- gives permission for and releases ministry.
- has integrity. People trust him.
- opens up his life as an example for people.
- does not seek to control and manipulate people.
- leads by motivation not intimidation.
- has a sense of purpose and is driven by that sense of purpose.
- casts a vision for those he leads.

The pastor is the key to multiplication in a church. He casts the vision for multiplication for the whole church.

He is the spiritual "mustard seed" for the entire ministry.

Multipliers multiply. God is not into division. Division comes when a leader seeks to split the church, urging some of the people to follow him instead of God. Division always reduces the circle of love.

Legalism is a primary tool of division. Legalistic leaders seek to find ways to exclude instead of to include people in a circle of love. Multipliers believe that people grow by being discipled and nurtured instead of by being judged and excluded.

Many of the people who now head up our ministries in Phoenix and Los Angeles were once considered problem-makers. Yet, if we had not included them in our circle of love, they would have been lost to the kingdom of God and their ministries would never have been released. Let me give you just a few examples.

Larry Kerychuk, who started our Master's Commission and now ministers to athletes, was a former pro-football player. When I first arrived in Phoenix, he shared his vision to reach athletes, teach them, get them filled with the Holy Spirit and send them back out to do ministry. I thought the vision he had seemed too big. Larry was a wild visionary with unrealistic dreams. But instead of thinking of all the reasons we could not do the ministry and of ways to exclude people, we prayed and dreamed.

The first conference for athletes was held with fifty people. But today that ministry has grown to an attendance of more than seven hundred at the conferences and plans have been drafted and funds earmarked to build a world-class training center. Many of America's leading Christian athletes have found Christ at the conferences.

I live the vicarious life through Larry and Bill Wilson and so many others whom we have released into ministry. No solitary leader can begin to do all that is needed for his or her church to grow. But when we live the vicarious life, including people in God's circle of love, then we begin to release ministry and see the church multiply beyond our wildest expectations.

Factor #2
Leaders multiply themselves and live the vicarious life

Ask yourself:

- Do I enjoy releasing others and seeing them prosper in ministry?
- Is my church willing to include people in God's circle of love in order to grow ministries and multiply?

Pray...

— to be filled with joy when others prosper in ministry.

— to release others into ministry.

— to live the vicarious life.

ADOPT A BLOCK

God has given me an idea to reach this community. I'm going to call it, "Adopt a Block."

My son, Matthew, co-pastor of the Los Angeles International Church, chose twenty blocks around the church for weekly visitation teams to call on the people in their assigned block every week.

Every Saturday morning each team, led by a "block head," goes out to tell people about the church and pray with people. Then they ask, "Is there anything we can do to help you?"

Sometimes they mow the grass, clean windows or baby-sit while a mother runs an errand. Once all the visits are made on a block, the team picks up all the trash and completely cleans up the area.

A few months after this ministry began, Matthew publicized the start of a new Hispanic church in the L.A.I.C. building. On the first Sunday morning Matthew looked outside to see who might be coming. "It looked like a convoy of people was pouring out of those houses," he told me. They had almost five hundred people in the first service. Today it continues to multiply in size.

A church was planted and many have been saved because Christians went out to love and network with people in their neighborhood.

Factor #3

People Touched by God

> And Saul also went home to Gibeah; and there went with him a band of men, whose hearts God had touched (1 Sam. 10:26).

Consider the first time you won a race, made a perfect score on a test or reached your highest goal. What did you do after that? I have exciting news. Beyond your highest mountain lies a higher peak. Above your greatest accomplishment rises one greater. Outdistancing your longest run stretches a longer marathon.

Saul had just been anointed king by Samuel. On the surface, becoming king could be regarded as the crowning event of life. But *being king* reaches far beyond simply being crowned king. Though anointed, Saul would discover that *being king* required far more than any oil poured upon him or any words spoken over him by Samuel. How could Saul hope to attain greater things in life than a coronation?

I especially love the last five words of this Scripture passage: "whose hearts God had touched." These exciting words burst with possibilities.

The potential for multiplication produced by men or women who have been touched by God is infinite.

When you surround yourself with people whose hearts

have been touched by God, an explosion shatters the status quo with exponential creativity and change. A high-octane denotation of human potential ignited by the raging fire of the Holy Spirit will produce a spiritual awakening that recreates Pentecost. Anything can take place when you are surrounded by people whose hearts have been truly touched by God.

God's touch resembles a lit match touching gasoline, a bolt of lightening striking an oil tanker or a grenade exploding inside a storage shed of dynamite. His touch does more than start something.

I hear people pray, "O God, just start something. Let the Holy Ghost come on down." I wonder if they know what they are asking. More than that, I would love to witness their responses when God does what they asked. When people who have been touched by God gather together, they are asking for more than virtual reality. When two or more gather in His name, God Himself shows up. Those whose hearts are touched by God are like kindling wood ready to burst into flame at the first touch of fire.

It is no wonder that fire broke out among the hundred and twenty saints gathered in His name at that first Pentecost. They had been touched by God in such a way that they were "spiritual kindling wood" just awaiting a spark. Do you want to spread like a raging wildfire, sweeping through everything in the path? Gather together those touched by God, and become kindling just waiting for Him to set you off! When God touches you — the sparks will fly!

No sacrifice is too great for men and women whose hearts God has touched.

Whatever God commands, they say, "Let's do it." Saul was anointed to lead. Are you called and anointed to be a leader? Then follow Saul's first step — surround yourself with those touched by God. If you are bored, they will excite you. If you are depressed, they will lift you up. If you are lost, they will guide you. If you are hurt, they will comfort you. If you are ready to go, they will go with you. Now that is truly exciting!

Jesus surrounded Himself with a group of men whose hearts were touched by Him. Because of the touch of God on their lives, the Bible says they literally turned the world upside down (Acts 17:6).

People whose hearts have been touched by God have the potential of righting the toppled world around them. We need such men and women. Our nation needs to be shaken and turned right side up by revival. We need people touched by God who will go out and change the world around them.

Factor #3
Surround yourself with men and women touched by God.

Ask yourself:

- Are those around you touched by God?
- Do they lift you up and not let you down?
- What will you do to pray for them and to affirm them?

Factor #3

- How will you avoid people who tear you down instead of build you up in the Lord?

Pray...

— that God will send you leaders and workers whom He has touched.

— for His touch daily in your own life.

— that God's touch will bring boldness to you and shake your world.

— for His touch to turn the world around you upside down.

FACTOR #4

Avoid Wrong Associates

> Blessed is the man that walketh not in the counsel of the ungodly, nor standeth in the way of sinners, nor sitteth in the seat of the scornful (Ps. 1:1).

Jesus surrounded himself with a group of men untouched by anything that the world had to offer. Those touched by the world are described in Psalm 1 as being wicked, skeptical and mocking. Such people pull down those around them to their level instead of lifting others up to a higher level. So be careful about those with whom you associate.

Steer a broad course away from critical, negative, skeptical people.

Negative people drain your energy and creativity. If you are conforming to Christ's image, then you can say to those around you, with Paul, "Follow my example, as I follow the example of Christ" (1 Cor. 11:1, NIV).

If your associates cannot follow your positive example by conforming to Christ, then they need to take a leave of absence from leadership. Ask them to dedicate time to prayer, the Word and Christian servanthood. Invite them to meditate on thoughts that create a Christ-like attitude in their lives as instructed in Philippians 4:8:

- whatsoever things are true,
- whatsoever things are honest,
- whatsoever things are just,
- whatsoever things are pure,
- whatsoever things are lovely,
- whatsoever things are of good report;
- if there be any virtue,
- and if there be any praise,
- think on these things.

If those around you work at conforming you to their image, then change your associates. The only image you should be changing into is Christ's image. His image reflects humility and servanthood (Phil. 2:5-8).

It takes boldness to make changes. "And when they had prayed, the place was shaken where they were assembled together; and they were all filled with the Holy Ghost, and they spoke the word with boldness" (Acts 4:31). The early Christians surrounded themselves with those whose hearts had been touched by the Holy Spirit.

Their lives shook the place where they were and boldly changed the world around them. "Now when they saw the boldness of Peter and John, and perceived that they were unlearned and ignorant men, they marveled; and they took knowledge of them, *that they had been with Jesus*" (Acts 4:13, italics added). As a result of being changed by association with Jesus, those early church leaders turned world history upside down. Those touched by God in the first-century church set in motion a chain reaction of changed lives from that day to the present.

In the early church, Christians spent time associating with one another as they became Christ-like. As a result, they influenced the world instead of the world influencing them. They multiplied themselves. We duplicate in others what we are. "And in those days, when the number of disciples were multiplied..." (Acts 6:1). Disciples reproduced disciples.

The possibilities are limitless with a band of men and women whose hearts have been touched by God. D. L. Moody said:

"It is yet to be seen what God can do with men or women who will yield themselves completely to God."

Through D. L. Moody, God touched thousands of men and women in America and England. It has been said that Moody raised up America in one hand and England in the other. He held both up to God and brought revival. Moody's changed life was multiplied in the lives of thousands, just as the early disciples' changed lives were multiplied.

A song we used to sing when I was a kid in high school went something like this: "Give me some men who are strong-hearted men, who'll fight for the right they adore. Starting with ten who are stouthearted men and I'll soon give you ten thousand more. Shoulder to shoulder and boulder to boulder they march as they go to the foe. There's nothing in this world that can mar the plans when stouthearted men meet together as men to men."

I like that song. It extols what stouthearted people can do. Avoid fainthearted men as your closest associates, for what they can accomplish pales in significance to what stouthearted men touched by God will achieve. They can do all things through Christ! (Phil. 4:13).

Factor #4
The wrong associates can do much more to damage your ministry than the enemy.

Ask yourself:

- Can my associates see my Christ-like example?
- Do they follow my example, or do they follow the world?
- What am I willing to do about those around me who are negative and critical?
- How will I avoid negative associates in the future?

Pray...

— for God to raise up people around you who are hungry for His presence.

— for the gift of discernment so that you will choose leaders and associates that follow your Christ-like example.

— that you will speak the truth in love to negative associates so that God will move them from influencing you to a place where Christ can touch and change their lives into His image.

A TRANSFORMED LIFE!

Tyrone James, who lived on Skid Row in downtown Los Angeles, shares his story: "I was filled with hatred and mixed up in alcohol, drugs, violence and gang banging. I came here for a meal. I treated them [the staff] terrible, even threatening Pastor Matthew with a gun. But even though I wanted to kill him, Pastor Matthew still treated me nice.

"After a while, it got to me, and I got on my knees and asked God to help me. I was at the point of suicide. You see, I had AIDS, and I thought my life was over. Pastor Matthew convinced me to go to a rehab place outside of San Francisco.

"I left all the street stuff behind and got into the Bible, fellowship and church for four months straight. I've seen changes in my life.

God has given me one last chance. And I'm not going to blow it.

"I'll never get over how God used the people I hated and wanted to kill to love me and lead me to Jesus."

Tyrone James returned to the Dream Center to thank all the pastors and staff for showing him the love of Jesus. He is now multiplying that love to his family with whom he is residing for the first time in two years.

Factor #5

Be Call-Driven — Not Burden-Driven

> Ye have not chosen me, but I have chosen you, and ordained you, that ye should go and bring forth fruit, and that your fruit should remain: that whatsoever ye shall ask of the Father in my name, he may give it you (John 15:15).

> ...your old men shall dream dreams" (Joel 2:28; Acts 2:17).

Be call-driven not burden-driven. Did you ever stop to think that most people accept the call of God when they have a burden? No one should ever accept the call because of a burden. Why? Because a burden will come, and a burden will go. But a call is always there.

Many are burdened to go overseas or to the inner city, but almost no one is called to go to Palm Beach, Florida, for ministry. We are so burdened for God in the crises areas of the world. Burdens will come and go but the call of God is forever. We can be called by God to dream dreams right where we are as well as dreams for the disaster areas of the world. God called me and gave me dreams for Phoenix. So when the alarm goes off tomorrow morning at 5:00 A.M. I will wake up to pray.

Now I don't have a burden at 5:00 A.M. For some people getting out of bed early in the morning to pray would be a terrible burden. They would moan from the moment the alarm sounded through the final amen of intercession.

When that's the case, early morning prayer is not a calling but a burden. Do not be burden-driven.

What gets me up at five o'clock in the morning? It's God's call and His dreams for me in Phoenix. What keeps me going when opposition comes against me? The call. What keeps me going when I don't feel like preaching? It's the call. I've been chosen by Jesus Christ. I've been set aside, sanctified and anointed by the Anointed One. The Bible says that even before I was born God anointed me, set me aside and ordained me (Ps. 139:15-16; Jer. 1:5).

When the heart has been touched by God, a person following His call is driven and motivated by supernatural power and strength.

When we obey His calling, we desire to do things we have never imagined. We are free to accomplish things that our minds and bodies could never have released us to do. We have a driving compulsion to serve God which springs out of His call, not our burdens for the world.

Be Driven By God's Dreams

When you are call-driven, you dream new dreams — God's dreams. I certainly have new dreams. They give me a reason to keep going on with God. Acts 2:17 promises, "And it shall come to pass in the last days, saith God, I will pour out of my Spirit upon all flesh: and your sons and daughters shall prophesy, and your young men shall see visions, and your old men shall dream dreams." *Old men* does not refer to chronological age but to spiritual maturity. Those who have been growing in faith and walking in God's Spirit will experience His dreams in their hearts. What dream has God deposited within you that drives you forward into His plans? Are you dreaming His new dreams or desperately trying to grasp fleeting wisps of stale, private aspirations?

My dreams are never my possessions. They both come from and belong to God. The wise lad Joseph recognized that as he sat in an Egyptian prison. Remember how his brothers hated his dreams and consequently, hated him? "Here comes that dreamer," they would say with disgust and scorn. Even though his brothers hated him and Potiphar threw him into prison, Joseph held onto his dreams. Why? Because he understood that both the dreams and their interpretations belonged to God (Gen. 40:8). Since they belonged to God, Joseph's dreams were an eternal possession that no temporal circumstance could distort or destroy.

Human dreams are always subject to the ebb and flow of life's ups and downs. But not God's dreams. They rise above trials and tests. They give direction to our lives and purpose to our plans. Joseph had every reason to be driven by his burdens. But he chose to trust God's dreams.

You can always assume burdens which will drag you and your ministry down to the pits. I encourage you to be driven by God's dreams for you, not by burdens.

Factor #5
Let God's call and dreams,
not your burdens, drive you.

Ask yourself:

- Do you know God's call upon your life?
- Have His dreams for you been revealed?
- Are you driven by His call and dreams or by your burdens?
- What will you do to release your burdens to Him?

Pray…

— to hear clearly God's call for your life.

— to see clearly His dreams for you.

— to release your burdens to Him.

— to become driven by His call and dreams.

Factor #6

Respect God's Dreams

> But Jesus beheld them, and said unto them, With men this is impossible; but with God all things are possible (Matt. 19:26).

God's dreams are bigger than me. What catches me up into ever rising currents of hope and power is God's dream for me and His church. How do I know it's God's dream and not simply my own fabrication or wishful thinking? I know it's God's dream when the dream is bigger, larger and greater than me. What do I mean? Paul captures it this way: "Now unto him [Christ] that is able to do exceeding abundantly above all that we ask or think, according to the power that worketh in us" (Eph. 3:20). His dreams are beyond my abilities. For a dream to be conceived and accomplished, it must be His and not mine. His dreams stretch far beyond human possibilities into the realm of impossibility.

God's dreams are impossible without Him. If I can fulfill a dream myself or if the church can accomplish one alone, then we do not need God. But if the dreams are impossible and exceed anything we can do or think, then we not only need God but must totally depend upon Him. When His dream materializes, we can never take the credit or glory for its realization. All glory for God's dreams belongs to Him, for only God has the power to accomplish His dreams.

God's dreams cannot be put off, ignored or forgotten. Not only am I unable to accomplish His dreams, I am also unable to procrastinate and to postpone them. When God gave our congregation the dream of the Los Angeles International Church, or L.A.I.C., He gave us a dream impossible to accomplish without a miracle from Him. That dream was bigger than us. The Los Angeles International Church is housed in a building that is bigger than our church. It's so big that now our friends and preachers in other churches all over America are coming to help us. Why? Because they are convinced that it's not Tommy Barnett's dream — it's God's dream. We call this work, "The church America is building." And it's a big dream that is impossible to postpone or ignore. We are compelled by God to act and to work with others in the body of Christ to see His dream accomplished.

God's dreams are captivating. They will not let me go. When my heart has been touched by God, nothing is too big, and no hurdle too great. How do you or I know that dream is from God? Sometimes when God gives you the dream, you want to let it go — it scares, overwhelms and astonishes you. If it's God's dream you cannot let it go.

Dreams often seem to progress along a certain path. At first we grasp our dreams fearing we might lose sight of them. But later the dreams are so filled with God's Spirit and power that they grasp us and will not let us go. In the midst of a pit, slavery and prison, Joseph's dreams from God did not abandon him. They stayed with him, lighting the darkest night and giving hope in the bleakest circumstance. When fulfilled, God's dreams give God glory.

Even before their fulfillment, God's dreams give light and inspiration to see His way even when all around you is discouraging and depressing.

God's dreams are like a cloud by day and a pillar of fire by night. Remember how Israel was led through the wilderness by God's cloud? Dreams are like that. Today you do not have a cloud, but you do have the Holy Spirit. And when He pours His Spirit upon you and gives you a dream, that dream becomes like a pillar of fire going before you to light the way. Follow God's dream through whatever wilderness you may traverse. His dreams remind you that He is present. He will never leave you nor forsake you (Heb. 13:5; Deut. 31:6).

God's dreams are holy. I treat God's dreams as I treat Him. When your heart has been touched by God, you treat His dream the way you treat Him. For example, you may have a pageant that acts out Jesus' birth so that the unsaved can see His love for them. Treat the pageant as a dream that God has given to reach people for His glory. Treat anything that God dreams with the same reverence with which you treat Him.

Treat the worship service as you treat God. Treat the music as you treat God. Have the ushers treat people as they would treat God. The bus drivers should run the bus route and the cameramen should operate the cameras with excellence. Every detail that fulfills God's dream is to be done with excellence as unto the Lord (Rom. 14:8).

Be careful to understand what I am saying. The dream

does not become an idol. But His dream is holy because He is holy, and it is to be respected because He is respected. The ark was not God, but it was treated with reverence because it came from God. So it is with His dreams. Too often God gives us a precious dream to be implemented, but we regard it with casual indifference and thus lose it. Cherish God's dreams and all the details for putting into action those dreams for you and your church.

Factor #6
Treat God's dreams the way you treat God.

Ask yourself:

- Will I treat His dreams as I treat Him?
- Can I stop procrastinating and move forward in His call?
- Will I go when He says go and wait when He says wait?

Pray...

— that His dream will grasp you and propel you into His future.

— that every detail of His dream will be done with excellence.

— that His dream will light your nights and inspire you in the tough times.

Dream God's Dream At Any Age

How well I remember Brother Bore, perhaps the greatest hospital visitor in the world. At ninety-one years of age, he had visited over six thousand people and led over one thousand people to Jesus Christ in one year.

Because he was sick with diabetes, doctors had suggested amputating his legs years earlier. He seemed to be plagued with every problem in the world. But do you know what kept Brother Bore alive? This dear man of God focused on God's dream not his problems. Most people his age had retired twenty-five years before, but his dream kept him alive and active for the Lord.

Brother Bore dreamed of visiting every hospital patient in every hospital in his town.

You can dream God's dream at any age. You are never too old nor too young to be used by God.

And after you realize one dream, God will give you another. You never retire from serving the Lord.

You will never be too old to dream His dreams and see miraculous, multiplication results.

What dream will God have for you at seventy, eighty or ninety years of age? Say "Yes" to His dream for you.

Factor #7

Be Motivated by God's Purpose

> But seek ye first the kingdom of God, and his righteousness; and all these things shall be added unto you (Matt. 6:33).

When your heart has been touched by God, you are no longer goal-oriented — you are purpose-oriented. Yes, I have goals, but they are in submission to and directed by His purpose. I fall short of some of my goals. Often my plans splatter upon the pavement of life. I get discouraged and want to quit and die. But if I'm purpose-oriented, even when my goals fail, I know what my purpose is.

Purpose takes me beyond my goals. Goals may have to be altered, changed or even relinquished. But purpose always keeps me on track.

When we have been touched by God, we know that our purpose is to glorify and love God as we carry out His will. When we stop short of His purpose and find ourselves oriented to managing life only by goals and objectives, we lose sight of our reason for doing ministry and become mired in details, policies and procedures. Then people will be sacrificed on the altar of policies, and methods will replace being led by His Spirit. Leaders who are only goal-oriented have their meetings, make their plans and then pray to seek God's blessing.

But those who are purpose-oriented discover that seeking first His Kingdom and righteousness will drive them to prayer (Matt. 6:33). In prayer, the purpose-driven leader desires to hear God's voice above all else. Recall that God's voice to Elijah was a gentle whisper. Why? The voices of the world and our own selfish desires will always be louder than His voice. His desire is that we silence every other voice and listen only to His. "Be still, and know that I am God" (Ps. 46:10). Only when we are still before Him and listening to His voice will we hear His purpose for our ministry and service.

Once we have listened to Him, then we can move ahead with setting goals and establishing objectives.

Too often we rush to serve God before we worship Him and spend time in His presence.

Like Cain, we offer God the sacrifice we have chosen to accomplish our selfish goals instead of seeking first His purpose (Gen. 4:3).

Purpose Is Motivated By Love

When your heart has been touched by God's purpose, you are filled with a new kind of love. It is a love for God and for others.

Wouldn't it be wonderful if we would learn just to love one another? Our motivation is this: "Let brotherly love continue" (Heb. 13:1). We do not set goals to love one another. Rather, our goals come from a purpose rooted in love to glorify God.

I have seen leaders enlist people into ministry to fulfill a goal of getting them more committed to loving and serving God. We may reason this way: *Let's make Brother Jones an usher in order to get him more involved in ministry or more active in the church.* Our goal is to enlist the efforts of Brother Jones, believing that he will learn to love and serve God more if he works as an usher. To our surprise, Brother Jones makes a terrible usher. He frowns at people and acts terribly burdened by his responsibilities. Why? He is goal-oriented, not purpose-oriented. He is not ushering out of His love for God but because we have asked him to work. We have not heard from God about a purpose for his ushering. We have simply set a goal to put him to work in the church. Before Brother Jones can minister, he must first love God and purpose to glorify Him in all that he does.

When your heart has been touched by God, you are filled with a new kind of love for your family and for your fellow man. This new kind of love is not conditional. Purpose motivated by unconditional love says, "No matter what happens to me...no matter who notices...no matter how long it takes...no matter how ungrateful others may be toward me, my purpose to glorify God and love Him and others will not change."

God's Purpose Fills You With Joy

With this new kind of love there comes a new kind of joy. "Your joy no man taketh from you" (John 16:22). Joy is rooted in loving God as you live in His purpose. You actually learn to enjoy the trip. The journey becomes more exciting than the destination as you go for the gold that God has purposed in your heart. Because He is with you on this trip, every day with Jesus is sweeter than the day before. You no longer dread reaching your goal because of a fear that God will be finished with you when you arrive at the finish line.

When you reach God's goals, His purpose within you inspires other dreams, more goals and greater journeys. You will never catch all the dreams He has for you because His purpose is filled with limitless dreams.

Imagine a cage filled with beautiful butterflies. Then imagine that each butterfly represents a dream. Your purpose is to catch a butterfly and release it into the surrounding forest so that it can be free. Once that dream is released, joy fills your life, but there are still more butterflies waiting to be set free. It would take a lifetime to catch and release all of God's dreams for you.

God's purpose for you is infinite. His dreams for you are innumerable.

As you finish one race and cross the finish line, another race starts and another dream is launched. A cloud of witnesses from ages past cheers you on from the grandstands of heaven. Keep your eyes fixed on Jesus (Heb. 12:2).

Factor #7
Be motivated by God's purpose, not your goals.

Ask yourself:

- Do you set goals and ask God to bless them, or do you seek God's purpose through prayer?
- Are you motivated by love to serve God and others?
- Does His joy fill you as you purpose to serve Him?

MULTIPLICATION

Pray...

— that you will be purpose-oriented not goal-oriented.

— that love for God will motivate your ministry and service.

— that joy will fill your inner life.

Factor #8

Discover Inner Peace

> Be careful for nothing; but in every thing by prayer and supplication with thanksgiving let your requests be made known unto God. And the peace of God, which passeth all understanding, shall keep your hearts and minds through Christ Jesus (Phil. 4:6-7).

As God touches your heart, you'll also experience a different kind of peace. I know the storm is raging. I know the boat is sinking. But He's on board. You will not sink. How can you fail? Why worry on this journey? You may not know how He's going to take care of everything, but He has promised: "I am with you always" (Matt. 28:20).

I have peace in the worst storms. Even when I go through the valley of the shadow of death, I fear no evil. Why? Because I've been touched by God.

Nevertheless, life can sometimes get dangerous. One Sunday I received a call from my son, Matthew, and he said, "Dad, this is one of the greatest Sundays we've ever had."

"Well Son," I replied, "you tell me every Sunday is your greatest."

"But it was the greatest," he insisted. "The crowd was the biggest. The altar call was great. And yet, Dad, I fought every demon in the world this week."

He began to tell me about all the battles he had fought that week. Then he commented, "This morning was the final thing. I preached from my heart, and conviction was there. I talked about how God can take a tattered life and mold it into something great. A man who had made a threat to me as I walked to my car after the Thursday night service was in the service today."

This man had said to Matthew, "I'm dying with AIDS, and I would just like to let people know what it's all about. I'll make you a promise. I'm going to come up on the platform during the Sunday service, pull out a gun and kill myself to make a statement."

Sunday morning the man with AIDS came up to Matthew after worship and said, "I decided that simply killing myself is not going to make a big enough impression. So I'm going to shoot you and kill you on the platform and then kill myself." Then he pulled out a gun from his pocket.

Alarmed, I asked, "What did you do, Matthew?"

Matthew told me he had said to the man, "You can pull out that gun and put it to my head right now and blow my brains out. It's not going to hurt me. I'm just going to go to heaven. You can't scare me with heaven. But I'm concerned about you — you'll burn forever in hell if you do it."

The last thing the man said to Matthew was, "I promise that I will carry this through, for I have nothing to lose. I want to make a big statement when I die."

My son asked me what he should do. I said, "Maybe you should call the police and make them aware of this man. They probably know about him."

"But that won't stop the threat," Matthew responded.

And I counseled, "I don't know what to tell you to do, Matthew. I'm afraid to tell you to do this or that because I would advise you wrong. I don't know what to do." (For the miraculous end to this story see page 40.)

As I hung up the phone, I thought, *It's a dangerous world. But what can cause us to be willing to face dangers like that?* There are many things that we may fear or not want to face in this world. I don't want to live next door to an abortion doctor or some child molester. I'm saddened when I hear about starving babies the world over. My heart breaks when I read of young gang members being killed in Los Angeles. But I also have an instinct for self-preservation. I was born with it. My instinct tells me: "I must watch out for myself and for my children."

Yes, I'm concerned. I want to keep a bullet out of my own son's head. But there is one thing more frightening to me: Not obeying the great commission to go into all the world and preach the gospel to every creature. That's the hardest commandment that God has ever given because it may run contrary to my will to live.

How do I overcome my instinct for self-preservation at times when sharing the gospel puts my life or the lives of my loved ones in danger? First, I overcome fear with the cross, because the cross is where I died to my own self-will. When we lay down our lives on the cross, we start living for Jesus Christ and belonging to Him.

The second way I overcome my instinct for self-preservation is to love. The Bible says that perfect love drives out all fear (1 John 4:18). How can I fear that which I love? So I can go through the valley of the shadow of death in the heart of Zaire, in the inner city or in any place that I fear, because if I love God and others my fear will disappear.

When God touches your life, you receive a whole new perspective on life. No longer are you living for today or for tomorrow, but for eternity. When your heart has been touched by God, you have eternal values. Life is not just a few days; rather life is an entrance to a great eternity. It's only the lobby into the big auditorium. So all your values change, and you now have an eternal perspective.

When your heart has been touched by God, no fear can overcome you. Love overcomes fear.

Suddenly you love the things that God loves. You learn that God loves people, and you get a passionate love for people, never fearing what they can do to you. Men who have been touched by God have turned the world upside down. Martin Luther was just an ordinary man until one day he went to Rome in search of God. He crawled up the steps of a cathedral. And as He crawled up, he kept uttering a prayer, "The just shall live by faith. The just shall live by faith."

The Pope told him, "Martin Luther, we're going to kill you if you don't change the way you act."

Martin Luther doubled up his fist and said, "And I'll punch you in the nose." He loved God and feared no man, not even the most powerful man of his day. Love for God gave him inner peace and overcame every fear.

We could have anxiety for our children and the threats against their lives. We could fear man for what he might do to us. Instead, we follow God's leading and discover our perfect peace in His purpose.

Factor #8
Fulfilling God's purpose brings inner peace.

Ask yourself:

- Is there any anxiety or fear that is robbing you of inner peace?
- Whom do you need to love in order to overcome your fear?
- How will you surrender your fear and receive God's peace for your life?

Pray...

— that God's love within you will conquer every fear.

— that you will learn to love whomever you now fear.

— with thanksgiving for His peace to guard your mind and heart.

YOU CAN'T FIGHT LOVE

The love of God makes multiplication work in the inner city. Clayton Golliher was a missionary on the streets of Hollywood for seventeen years, reaching out to runaway kids on Hollywood Boulevard. He reached a lot of those kids — clothing, restoring and saving them. He knew that if he did not reach a runaway on the Hollywood streets within two weeks, then the pimps and drug dealers would probably hook the runaway into a life of prostitution and addiction.

In all those years of ministry, Clayton never had a place to house his runaways. When the Dream Center started, we said, "Clayton, come and join with us." Multiplication forms a network of love.

Now an entire floor of the Dream Center is devoted to housing runaways. Clayton tells us, "I get down on my hand and knees and kiss the ground every morning, thanking God for the Dream Center."

He gathers in multitudes of runaways, rescuing them from the streets and bringing them a new life in Christ.

Pimps and drug dealers chase him and curse his ministry. However,they cannot fight love. God's love is winning the war for souls on the streets of Los Angeles.

Factor #9

Don't Waste Your Time

For we walk by faith, not by sight (2 Cor. 5:7).

And he [Jesus] said unto them, This kind can come forth by nothing, but by prayer and fasting (Mark 9:29).

Churches multiply disciples only through supernatural faith. Supernatural faith that produces signs and wonders comes by prayer and fasting. There are four different levels of faith, and all of these levels are mediated by the Holy Spirit.

1. Saving faith. Paul said to the Philippian jailer, "Believe on the Lord Jesus Christ, and thou shalt be saved" (Acts 16:31). This is the level of faith that everyone born again in Christ has experienced.

2. Sanctifying faith. This faith enables us to grow in grace, live in holiness and walk in godliness. Sanctifying faith empowers you to be faithful in your daily walk with Christ.

3. Surpassing faith. This faith is motivated by God's purpose in your life. It inspires His dream in you. It's the kind of faith that caused Noah to build an ark on dry land. Surpassing faith caused Abram to leave his home and go to a promised land he had never seen. Those who find this faith enjoy a measure of God's power to accomplish things that are otherwise impossible.

But there is another level of faith we must aspire to if

the church is going to multiply.

4. Supernatural faith. Those who minister in supernatural faith believe in the day-to-day supernatural operation of the Holy Spirit. For them the Holy Spirit is not merely a one-time experience, but a daily walk with the person of the Holy Spirit. People who live in the supernatural believe in miracles. They depend on miracles. They recognize the need for miracles in their lives.

I know a pastor who asked all those in his congregation who needed a miracle to stand. Many stood but still more remained seated. He then addressed his remarks to those who had not stood. "Those who do not recognize their need for a miracle are those most in need of one." Walking by faith not by sight is a supernatural experience that allows us to encounter daily miracles.

Living by Supernatural Faith Confronts Satan

I believe that when we walk in the supernatural we become like Martin Luther. When he discovered the grace and power that come through living by faith and not by works, he faced the enemy. As he battled the devil in his room, Luther took an ink bottle and threw it at the devil. It hit the wall, broke, splattered and left an ink spot. When the workers came to paint his wall, he wouldn't let them do it. He left the ink blot on his wall to remind him that there is a supernatural devil that powerfully opposes faith.

As the early church manifested the supernatural power of God, it multiplied in numbers. "And the word of God increased; and the number of the disciples multiplied in Jerusalem greatly" (Acts 6:7). Years ago, I got on my knees and prayed, "O God, I'm not going to be a preacher if I'm not going to be real. I'm not going to be a sham. I'm not going to waste my life on something that's superficial."

Superficial faith never grows a church. Only supernatural faith can empower a church to multiply its numbers and ministries.

I determined in my ministry: "I'm not going to waste my life on something that is not miraculous." When people come to our church, they have supernatural faith and expect the miraculous.

If we want the supernatural instead of the superficial in our ministries, then we must follow God's methods and ways. His ways will lead us into direct confrontation with the devil. What is required for such a confrontation? What leads to supernatural faith?

Our nation needs churches filled with pastors who know God, walk with God and spend time in prayer and fasting, pleading for supernatural signs and wonders which will lead the lost to Christ and multiply the church.

As a young man years ago, I went to Calcutta, India. There I met Mark Buntain. He was in the midst of a nervous breakdown. He would cry all day over the burdens of his city. He said he felt those burdens were like a band around his head, killing him.

As I was on my way out of the country driving to the airport with Mark, I said, "Mark, would you let me pray for you?" He said, "Please do." I put my hand on his head and said, "O God, I am not much but I want to honor Your Word. Your Word says that in Jesus' name you will set the captives free. Cause this band to loose, God." He started the car and said, "I feel better; my head is not tight."

Later Mark Buntain wrote in his book, *St. Mark of Calcutta*, that a great hospital in India was built and thousands of people were fed every day. He also wrote that if God had not supernaturally healed him that day through the prayers of a young, twenty-one-year-old evangelist, his ministry never would have multiplied.

If the church is to see continual, multiplication growth, greater signs and wonders, and the tearing down of Satan's strongholds, it must have a supernatural faith that prays and fasts.

Factor #9
Don't waste your time on the superficial:
Live in supernatural faith that prays and fasts.

Ask yourself:

- Is my faith moving beyond the superficial to the supernatural?
- Am I willing to pray and fast in order to confront the devil and the world?
- Does my faith produce signs and wonders that lead the unsaved to Jesus?

Factor #9

- Will I continue in prayer and fasting to see God's mighty works in my life and church?

Pray...

— that your faith will grow to supernatural proportions as you trust God for miracles.

— that your willingness to pray and fast will grow.

— that signs and wonders will follow your faith, leading the lost to Christ.

— that you will not waste time on the superficial but will seek supernatural faith through prayer and fasting.

Factor #10

Be a Soul-Winning Church

> They that were scattered abroad went everywhere preaching the word (Acts 8:4).

Years ago a lady said to me, "Pastor Barnett, our church is big enough. Let's not go after any new people." Later this lady, with great excitement, said to me, "Sunday my son is coming to visit. Preach real good — I want him to get saved."

And I answered, "But sister, the church is big enough!"

Then bowing her head, she replied, "Pastor, I believe we have room for one more."

"And the Lord added to the church daily such as should be saved" (Acts 2:47). Every day the Lord added to the church. The New Testament tells us that the minimum number of converts a church should win to Christ is 365 per year! However, out of a quarter of a million churches in America, very few ever reach this New Testament minimum. I am often asked, "Is there anything wrong with a church being small?" My reply is, "No, not for a week, but if a church is truly a New Testament church, it must grow daily."

How did the New Testament church accomplish this feat? They did it in the temple *and* in the villages. Yet today our churches often try to win the lost by reaching people only in the church building, the "temple." How can a church average at least one convert a day? This way: *Its members must win souls every day.* Only personal evangelism can accomplish this feat.

When I came to serve my first church in Davenport, Iowa, I had a dream to see a great soul-winning church built for God. Every week I would challenge my congregation to go out and bring the lost to church. I would preach my heart out, give wonderful illustrated sermons and then give an altar call. As the people saw their loved ones saved, their faith grew, and they continued to bring more unsaved people to church. During special services as many as one hundred people would accept Christ. Our church was growing.

Then one day I read a report that 80 percent of the unconverted would not go to a church under any circumstance. Therefore I concluded that if the unsaved would not come to us, we must go to them. For when we go to them, our audience is limited only to the number of people alive in our generation.

We Must Take God Out and Bring People In

Unfortunately, much of evangelism in the twentieth century has been built on the philosophy that if we build a beautiful building at a good location, the unchurched will come. Yet when we study some of the largest churches in America, we discover that location has the least bearing of any factor in the growth of a church.

Nowhere in the Bible does it tell the unsaved to go to church. But we the church have been commanded by God's Word to "go out into the highways and hedges, and compel them to come in, that my house may be filled" (Luke 14:23). The last command that Jesus gave in the book of Matthew was to go into all the world to save the lost (28:19-20).

Consider this: There have been great evangelistic churches in our country for years that have operated on the principle of filling up the church with the lost and having a great preacher proclaim, "You must be born again." Such churches believe that evangelistic preaching in the church will win the lost. But evangelistic churches operate under a misconception.

A New Testament church is *not* an evangelistic church — a New Testament church is a soul-winning church. A soul-winning church is one in which the members come to be strengthened and edified so that they may go out and preach the gospel to a dying world.

A soul-winning church may not have as good a preacher as an evangelistic church, but it will reach far more people. It is not my job as a pastor to win souls. It is my job as a Christian to win souls. As a pastor, I am to work on my congregation to get them in shape to go out and minister the good news of salvation to the world.

In Davenport God began to teach me that new Christians needed to be equipped to be soul-winners. The pastor must reproduce and multiply himself or herself in each person sent out from the church.

Each soul-winner reaches people who need Christ but who never would come to a church service.

Thus Christians go out into the world to witness to their unsaved friends, neighbors and coworkers.

The results in Davenport and later in Phoenix were phenomenal. Revival broke loose. At times, during a single altar call over one thousand people were saved. Greater numbers of people today are answering the altar calls on Sunday but even more are being saved during the week as our people are winning them to Christ in all locations of our city: in factories, homes, prayer meetings, Bible studies, jails and convalescent homes; on the streets and through bus and counseling ministries.

Years ago I thought that the battle for souls was won or lost when the sun went down on Sunday night. In reality, the battle is won or lost when the sun goes down on Saturday night. What we do during the week determines what happens on Sunday. Now I realize that soul-winning is a daily activity of sowing the good news into the lives of people. Whatever happens on Sunday is only part of the harvest that occurs daily.

Prayer releases the Word of God; praise releases the presence of God; and work releases the power of God. That Word must be shared daily throughout our cities.

When I am asked, "When is a church big enough?" my reply is, "When everyone in our city has accepted Christ. Then and only then is the church big enough."

Factor #10
A New Testament church is not an evangelistic church; it's a soul-winning church.

Ask yourself:

- What is your church doing to equip people to win the lost?

- What is expected of the pastor in your church in regard to evangelism and equipping?
- Are you personally witnessing to others about Christ daily?

Pray...

— for pastors to fulfill their personal responsibility to be soul-winners and to equip the body to win souls daily.

— for Christians to witness daily to the unsaved in all walks of life.

Illustrated Sermons Help a Church Multiply

For years I have used illustrated sermons to highlight the gospel for people in our churches.

In one illustrated sermon, I preached about the rapture. At various intervals, I had the spotlight shift to people who were pulled out of their seats up into the ceiling by thin wires. At the end of the sermon, I was also pulled up. As I slowly ascended, I asked, "Are you going to be left behind?"

Recently while using the metaphor of wrestling, I preached an illustrated sermon titled "The Empty Ring." In it I told the life story of professional wrestler Superstar Billy Graham, who is a member of my church; and of Jake the Snake who was recently saved. As I gave the altar call, over a thousand people came forward to accept Christ, including wrestler Big Bill Anderson and referee Jesse Hernandez.

Thousands of wrestling fans were saved through this method.

Anyone can use drama and simple props to help saved and unsaved people to understand the gospel. Jesus did the same thing when He told parables.

FACTOR #11

Prioritize Right

> Therefore shall a man leave his father and his mother, and shall cleave unto his wife: and they shall be one flesh (Gen. 2:24).
>
> And thou shalt teach them [God's commandments] diligently unto thy children, and shalt talk of them when thou sittest in thine house, and when thou walkest by the way, and when thou liest down, and when thou risest up (Deut. 6:7).

I put God and people as the first priority in my life because Jesus says, "Inasmuch as ye have done it unto one of the least of these my brethren, ye have done it unto me" (Matt. 215:40). When I serve others in Jesus' name, I am putting first the kingdom of God and His righteousness. I have always taught our people that the only way we can minister to the Lord is through people. Praise and worship can become somewhat selfish if it does more for me than it does for God. True worship begins when I go out and win people to Jesus Christ, minister to the handicapped and take care of the hurting widows.

My children love the ministry. They love people. They can't wait to go to church. Their lives are built around the church because I have taught them that to love and minister to God is to love and minister to people.

For example, one Christmas as we were getting ready to open our presents, I received a phone call from the family of a man who was dying in the hospital, asking me to come immediately. "Look, I need to go right now," I told my family. "Please understand. I know you hate to wait. I know you've been looking forward to this day. But God will honor and bless us when we care for people." My children have never resented the people or the church because they realize that ministry is *people!*

Let your family know that next to God and ministering to people in Jesus' name, they are number one. Do you realize that? Pastor or Christian leader, tell me about your life. How do you spend time with your family? Here are some simple ways I have discovered which make my family a priority over church and work and everything else in life except God. He gave me a family as a gift to cherish, love, nurture, spend time with and protect.

Spend time with your spouse and family. I go home every night at five o'clock. I do not bring other people home for dinner. I rarely go to evening meal functions. One day I stood before my church and said, "Either you can have a man of God for a spouse and parent or you can have a 'buddy'. Now if you want a man or woman of God, he or she must pray, read the Bible, study, spend time alone with God and spend time with family. Parents who keep their families together spend time with them. A 'buddy' spends time with everyone but his family. The family gets shortchanged." The primary way a spouse and parent demonstrates God's love to family is by spending time with family. Nothing substitutes for time.

The Lord spoke to me one day, "You need to block out Monday night for your grandchildren." So we all get together on Monday night and go out for dinner. We take the grandkids to rides or do something else great for them on that night. I intentionally schedule time for family.

Be interested in your family's interests. Go to all the kids' games and activities. I not only went to the games, I also went to the practices. They never had an award until I came along, but then every year at the little kids' banquet they'd give me an award for the most loyal father attending. My daughter ran track, and I believe the only reason she did is because she knew I loved it.

Set family guidelines. Here are the guidelines for our family. We never asked, "Are we going to church Wednesday night?" It was never questioned. On Wednesday night we went to church. We never had any division on that point. However, if there was a basketball or football game they were to play in, they'd come and say "Dad, I know church is more important than anything in the world. But would it be okay? This is an important basketball game." We'd sit down, and I'd say, "Look. I want you to know church is more important than anything, but I want you to be able to develop in these areas. Sure, I understand." And they would appreciate the fact that we understood the important events in life. I believe that parents should be understanding.

Be affectionate. Now, let me tell you. Each child is different, so show your affection in a way that each child can receive. Some love hugs. Others desire kisses. Some need a shoulder squeeze. And remember to express affirmation and appreciation. You will receive what you give. Teach them to love by loving them.

Teach them that people fail. When other people failed, my children said to me, "Look, Dad. You taught us all our lives that people are people. It doesn't mean they are bad — they just fail." When people make mistakes, I say,

"That's just people." Pastors or church leaders will often criticize others in the church. That has a very destructive effect on spouses and children. Just teach them that people are saved or unsaved. They are just people. And people are going to make mistakes. People are inconsistent. People in our church say, "Pastor, we don't have money, but we'll die for you. We'll be with you as long as you live." And the next week they are gone. People. That's people. Some people are loyal, and some are not. Don't put your trust in people. Just love and accept them (Rom. 15:1-7).

Teach your family that anything accomplished in ministry must be done through people.

For any success or prosperity I have enjoyed, I first gave glory to God and then acknowledged to the people that they had become good followers. It is important to love God's people.

Be true to your own principles. For example, one principle we have in the Barnett household is that Barnetts do not quit. That's right. We just do not quit. If we are friends, we are friends forever. There are some things that are inherited and passed down from generation to generation. I've taught my children the values we believe in with all our hearts. As a family, teach and follow God's absolute truths. Do not have relativistic values which change with every circumstance. Stand firm on God's truth.

Teach them when they fail to apologize. I learned that early. If you are wrong, just say, "I'm wrong. Forgive me."

Listen to the doubts and fears of one another. I encouraged my children to say, "Dad, I don't understand this about the ministry." Or, "Dad, would you help me in this area? I'm having a struggle."

Let family members know that you believe in them. Believe in them with all your heart. Believe that God is going to use them mightily in His kingdom.

A pastor friend said to me, "What difference does it make if I win the whole world to Christ but lose my wife and children?" He was speaking about priorities, about putting family before church, work, leisure and busyness.

Factor # 11
Next to God and people, your #1 priority is family.

Ask yourself:

- How do I show my family that they are my first priority in life and ministry next to God?
- How much time do I spend with my family daily?
- Which area of expressing love to my family do I need to grow in the most?

Pray...

— to implement many different ways you can express love to your family.

— to have wisdom to schedule time with your family.

Factor #12

Soul-Winning Is a Command

> Go ye therefore, and teach all nations, baptizing them in the name of the Father, and of the Son, and of the Holy Ghost (Matt. 28:19).

I was speaking at a church growth conference on the subject "Why All Christians Should Win Souls." A well-meaning pastor stood up and asked, "Brother Barnett, this is all well and good for you because you have the gift of soul-winning, but what about all those people who do not have this gift?"

Let me say emphatically, soul-willing is *not* one of the gifts of the Spirit. Rather it is the last command given to us by our Lord before He left this earth to ascend to His Father. Since it was His last word to us, it must have been His most important.

Of course, as members of the body of Christ, each of us has been given a certain function and granted specific gifts. However, we must not forget we are first of all soul-winners before anything else. You may say, "I am a deacon, and this is my ministry." No. You are first a soul-winner and second a deacon. You are first a soul-winner and then a teacher. You are first a soul-winner and then a pastor. The truth is you are not fully qualified to be a deacon, teacher or pastor if you do not win souls.

"The fruit of the righteous is a tree of life; and he that winneth souls is wise" (Prov. 11:30). The fruit of the godly life is leading others to Christ, and wisdom is the characteristic of the soul-winner. We may have academic degrees and great spiritual insights, know all the visions of Daniel, understand the beast of Revelation, and astound people with our Bible knowledge, yet in God's eyes we are wise when we win the lost.

Much has been written and said today about the need to minister to the Lord. We stress the importance of vocal praise unto the Lord. While this is important, we seem to miss one of the greatest ways we can minister to the Lord — telling others about His saving power.

One of the most exciting truths in Scripture is: God loved us so much that He chose to share with us the thing that is closest to His heart — reaching the unsaved. "For the Son of Man is come to seek and to save that which was lost" (Luke 19:10). He could have carried out His redemptive plan without us, but He chose instead to make us "workers together with Him" (2 Cor. 6:1).

There is only one reason why God leaves us on this wicked, sinful earth after we are saved. If it were to sing and shout alone, I could do that better on heaven's streets of gold. If it were to get deeper into the Word, I could do that better sitting at the feet of the apostles. We have been put on this earth for one reason, and that reason is found in Ephesians 2:10, "For we are His workmanship, created in Christ Jesus unto good works." What is the purpose of good works? To glorify God, thus witnessing to others about the saving grace of Jesus Christ.

Some say, "Pastor, I believe this is true, and I will pray about it to see if it is God's will for me to win souls."

We do not have to pray about soul-winning, as it was the last will and testament of our Lord before He ascended.

Others say, "I don't think that I would enjoy it." Let me ask you, what mother enjoys cleaning or washing clothes or changing a baby's diaper? They are jobs that must be done, and love demands it.

Since the spirit is willing but the flesh is weak, here are three things we can do to help us discipline our lives to win souls.

1. **Set a time to go soul-winning and stick to it.** Plan your weekly schedule so that it revolves around your soul-winning, not so your soul-winning revolves around your weekly schedule.

2. **Take someone with you,** preferably a new convert. It will teach him how to win souls. However, the main reason to take him is because you will be more likely to do a better job. Also, it is the way taught in the Bible — going two by two (Luke 10:1).

3. **Go and harvest.** Jesus said in Matthew 9:37: "The harvest truly is plenteous, but the laborers are few." Jesus is saying that the need today is not so much for sowers, but for reapers. The seed has been sown and is ripe. The successful soul-winner is the one who goes, led by the Spirit, with a purpose and a goal to lead people to Christ.

There are two women in my church who give one day a week to witnessing. Before they go, they always set a goal of how many people they want to lead to Christ. Recently they exceeded their goal and led over eighty people to

Jesus. These women are not merely exercising a divine gift from God. They are modern-day disciples of Jesus who believe that He meant what He said.

Factor #12
Soul-winning is a command — not a gift.

Ask yourself:

- Are you making excuses for not winning souls?
- To whom are you witnessing right now? When will you ask that person to accept Jesus Christ as Lord and Savior?
- Have you set a time in your schedule to pray for and witness to the lost each week?

Pray...

— for the power and boldness in the Holy Spirit to be a soul-winner.

— for someone who is lost and needs your witness of Jesus Christ.

— for other Christians to receive boldness to become soul-winners.

BIRTHED BY PRAYER

For two years, 1901-1902, faithful believers in the tiny nation of Wales prayed. Suddenly the Welsh people were electrified by the presence of the Lord. In just one month, thirty-four thousand were saved in Wales.

One Christian publication commented, "It is not a question of one town being awakened, but of the entire principality being on fire." God touched Wales in response to prayer.

Prayer was spirited, passionate and mighty. The men in one town formed a "Get out of the bed brigade." They prayed for God to wake men out of their beds and bring them to the prayer meeting so they could get saved. Within an hour men awoke mysteriously, got up and went down to the church to get saved by the power of God.

Church attendance rose by 90 percent. Church membership jumped to 75 percent of the population and in some places it was as high as 90 percent.

The *London Times* said, "It was something from another world." And that's what revival is. It is the sound of a mighty rushing wind.

Revival is something from another world.

And it all starts with prayer.

Factor #13

Birth Revival With Prayer

> If my people, which are called by my name, shall humble themselves, and pray, and seek my face, and turn from their wicked ways; then will I hear from heaven, and will forgive their sin, and will heal their land (2 Chr. 7:14).

In 1904 Wales needed revival perhaps more than many places on earth. Poverty-stricken Wales was a struggling mining region enveloped by darkness, profanity, immorality and greed. Though ignored by the general populace, the church of that day was already praying in earnest. Prayer had begun in 1901, and by 1902 two thousand prayer groups had formed all over the little country of Wales with its population of a million and a half people. Qualified ministers like G. Campbell Morgan, F. B. Meyers and Gypsy Smith were all there with potential to lead a revival. But God did not choose to use these men.

Instead the Holy Spirit anointed a twenty-five-year-old unknown Welsh coal miner by the name of Evan Roberts. Probably no other single person in modern history was so instrumental in the move of God as Roberts. Evan Roberts had worked twelve hours a day from the age of twelve. But while his young peers consumed their work breaks with swearing, smoking, drinking and chewing, he removed himself from their company to read Scripture.

For thirteen years Evan Roberts had prayed for a move of God's Spirit. Every time the church doors were open this young man was there on the front row. One year prior to the revival that flooded Wales, the Spirit of God broke through and washed over this young man. He prayed so loud and so hard that his landlady kicked him out of his apartment. Here was his prayer: *Bend me. Bend me. Bend me, O Lord.*

This young man was willing to pay the price. He sold everything he had to pay his bills. He even tried to pay others for the opportunity to preach. But the doors were closed to him until he went to his own pastor and asked, "Would you let me preach here?"

At first the pastor said, "No." But Evan kept begging until the pastor finally said, "If you are willing to stay after service on Wednesday and if anyone stays, you can preach to them." Seventeen stayed. He started by saying, "I have a message from God."

A man with a message from God can shake the world. Robert's message was simple. His message was concise. His message was anointed. Here's what it was:

1. You must confess every known sin to God and make right every sin known unto man.
2. You must remove doubtful habits from your life.
3. You must obey the prompting of the Holy Spirit.
4. You must go public with your witness for Jesus Christ.

When he finished his message, all seventeen people fell to their knees weeping before God. In just a few weeks, every church building in Wales was packed and hundreds were standing on the outside desiring to be inside.

Because Evan Roberts prayed, fasted and sought God,

he had a vision in 1904 that the revival would see a hundred thousand people saved in Wales and would literally sweep around the world. He was loudly ridiculed and scorned by religious leaders; nevertheless, within five months, the revival added a hundred thousand people to the church.

Religious people cannot quench a revival from God birthed by prayer.

The revival moved on to England and Ireland. The church added more than a million people to its rolls and at least that many more were reportedly saved. The revival swept through central Europe, Norway and Scandinavia. It spread down to Africa and India, through China and into Korea. Healings, visions, signs and wonders such as those recorded in the book of Acts were witnessed throughout the revival.

Incidentally, Korea is the only nation moved by this revival which has kept pace with the momentum of 1904. Reports say that at the turn of the century in Korea only 1 percent of Koreans were even nominal Christians while today one in two Koreans profess Christ. Some of the largest churches in the world are in Seoul, Korea.

I was invited to Seoul, Korea, to speak to Dr. Cho's forty-seven thousand deaconesses and three thousand deacons. They took me up to Prayer Mountain where an auditorium that seats ten thousand people was filled and an overflow crowd gathered in the basement. Everyone was on on his knees praying and crying out to God.

Why is Korea in revival? The answer is simple: prayer. Prayer has literally built the greatest church in the world.

Had there been no extraordinary prayer, there would have been no extraordinary awakening. John Wesley said, "It appears that God will do nothing except in response to people's prayers." That one little statement has affected me more than any I have heard about revival.

Factor #13
All revival is birth by prayer.

Ask yourself:

- Am I willing to pray and fast for revival for as long as it takes? Will I ask others to join me?
- Will I listen to God regardless of what others think or say?
- How will I personally respond to Evan Robert's simple message of revival?

Pray...

— and fast for revival in your church and city.

— that God will move mightily in our land.

— that you will be faithful to whatever the Lord has you to do in His revival.

FACTOR #14

Be a Permission-Giving Church

I dreamed of a church which would be a place where hurting people could come and get their needs met. I would say to the people, "I'm going to release you into ministry." Everybody in this church would find a need and seek to fill it.

Ministry and leadership are not about control but about release. Some in ministry are so controlling of others that ministry is stifled and inhibited. Their need to control makes them fearful and suspicious of others. As a result, they become like the steward who buried his talent in the ground (see Matt. 25:24-25). He certainly had perfect control over his resources, but nothing was accomplished for his master.

God does great things in churches where ministry is released. We call our church a *permission-giving church.* A permission-giving church says, "Go for it." It's not run by a group of people who sit around in a board meeting thinking of reasons why people cannot do ministry. It's run by saints who say, "If you want to work for God, *go do it.*"

Someone came up to me in our church and said, "Pastor, I'm a little offended. We don't have an Indian ministry in our church."

I said, "Do you know why? Because you haven't started one."

The way we start ministries is not to plan a ministry in a

meeting but to say, "Yes," when someone receives a dream from God for a ministry, comes to us and says "God has laid it upon my heart." That's the way ministries go forward.

I had always dreamed of having an international ministry. However, one of my associate pastors, Bill Wilson, went for that dream years before the Los Angeles International Church did. When he was the bus director in Davenport, he came to me and said, "Pastor, I must go to New York. I know you said you have always wanted to go there. And I'm just going to represent you and try to build a church there for the glory of God." I was so thrilled and excited to see him released for that dream. Now he has thousands of people involved in the ministry to God's glory.

I had a dream when I was eighteen years old to go to Los Angeles and build a church. After almost forty years of prayer and seeking God, that dream is becoming a reality. Years went by. As our church in Phoenix grew, I said to myself, "Well, it's never going to happen." Never mistake delay for denial. Waiting is God's means of preparation. As you are being prepared in God's waiting room don't allow discouragement to rob you of God's dream. At the right time, our church — filled with people who release ministry — said "Yes," and the Los Angeles ministry was released.

God has called us to be *seers* — those who can see God's dreams and vision as reality. Seers realize that there is a miracle in God's house.

A permission-giving church is filled with seers who are willing to become doers.

The negative and critical pew-sitters need to repent or go elsewhere. The seers see the invisible as visible and the things that are not as though they are. "We look not at the things which are seen, but at the things which are not seen: for the things which are seen are temporal; but the things which are not seen are eternal" (2 Cor. 4:18).

Too often we postpone our "Yes" to ministry and procrastinate about everything that would help us become a permission-giving church. If you just keep saying, "Yet a few more months," you will never possess the dream. In other words, we are always pushing "Yes" away from ourselves. *Faith is now.* Whatever you desire, when you pray, believe that you already possess it. Jesus would say to us, "Don't say, yet four months. Behold, I say unto you, 'Lift your eyes up now.'" He's saying, "By faith, see beyond the present natural circumstance into the supernatural purpose of God." Paul said, "We walk by faith, not by sight" (2 Cor. 5:7). At times, your only clear vision comes through the eyes of faith.

When darkness surrounds you, see what God has for you with the eyes of faith.

When I first went to Davenport I pastored seventy-six of the meanest Christians you've ever seen in your life. Just to get inspiration to preach I had to refer to that Scripture that says, "Be not dismayed at their faces" (Jer. 1:17). Often I had to preach with my eyes lifted up and closed. Sometimes you have to lift your eyes above the foreboding circumstances and the doubts of others. With your eyes fixed on the present circumstances, you will miss God's vision and allow hope to melt into despair.

"Hope deferred makes the heart sick" (Prov. 13:12, NAS). So do not defer your hope saying, "yet four months." Did you know you can die quicker of a broken heart then you can of a heart attack? You can simply lose the will to live because your heart has been broken over unfulfilled dreams and desires. People who are physically ill can recover if they have something to live for, but people who are heartsick and hopeless will welcome death because they have no reason to live. A vision can literally snatch them out of the jaws of death by declaring, "Not yet! You can't die because you have a dream to fulfill."

"But desire fulfilled is a tree of life" (Prov. 13:13, NAS). There is nothing that will bring vitality faster than seeing your dreams fulfilled. A dream will will keep you younger, healthier and more alive than anything else.

Inspiring leadership gives others permission to minister with their fullest, God-given potential. Such leadership is birthed from the knowledge that God has released those who desire to step out. Godly leadership has walked by faith trusting God's "Yes" in their own lives (see 2 Cor. 1:17-20). Released to hope and believe God's dreams for themselves, godly leaders release others into ministry.

Factor #14
Find ways to say Yes! to ministry: Be a permission-giving church

Ask yourself:

- Have you experienced God's "Yes" in your own life?
- Is your church a permission-giving church?
- Whom do you need to release into ministry?

MULTIPLICATION

Pray...

— to experience continually God's "Yes" in your life.

— to release others into ministry.

— for your church to grow as a permission-giving church.

THE FRENCH CONNECTION

One day Leo Godzich came to me and promised, "You will preach to more than three thousand French-speaking people next summer."

On a Saturday night the following summer, Leo called and said, "You will have to have somebody interpret in French during the service tomorrow. I told you there were going to be three thousand French-speaking people, but there are only two thousand."

Because we were willing to reach out to these people, God did an awesome work in their lives.

Sixteen hundred came forward that day to accept Christ. Leo baptized hundreds of them in the pond. Many of the people were unmarried couples who were living together. After he told them that they needed to get married, more than thirty couples got married during the service that evening.

Every year the corporation president in France brings his top distributors on vacation here and takes them to church. They have started couples' groups and Bible studies all over France.

One person, Leo Godzich, had a desire to reach out to the French. He became a "mustard seed" for multiplying disciples.

Factor #15

Know Where Your Attention Goes

> And Elisha said unto her, What shall I do for thee? Tell me, what hast thou in the house? And she said, Thine handmaid hath not anything in the house, save a pot of oil (2 Kin. 4:2).

When we focus our attention on problems, then all we can see is lack. A few years ago I decided that if I had the power from God to find a solution, I would. If God did not empower me at that moment, then I would work on it, pray about it, wait on God and seek positive input. But I would not dwell on the problem.

This widow in 2 Kings 4 could see only her problem — her lack. "Thine handmaid hath not anything in the house." Her attention focused on "nothing." However, the Bible asserts that faith is the "substance of things hoped for" (Heb. 12:1). Faith sees something instead of nothing:

- possibility instead of impossibility;
- potential instead of impotence;
- ability instead of inability;
- hope instead of despair;
- addition instead of subtraction;
- multiplication instead of division;
- increase instead of decrease;
- harvest instead of famine;
- substance instead of superficiality.

Remember, you cannot multiply with nothing. Zero times anything still results in zero. Elisha helped this woman discover what she did have — a pot of oil. Her attention shifted to what she had, and then God's power flowed to use what she had to meet her need.

One survey noted that most people have no vision for the next ten years. All they know is what they do not want. This negative vision of what people "do not want" becomes, unfortunately, the very thing that happens to them.

I talked with a pastor who had lost an enormous amount of money in a terrible investment. His wife asked, "What are you going to do?"

He replied, "I'm healthy, and I have a good mind. I've lost a fortune. But we have wonderful children, and we love each other. We have a great church and a great God. So I'm going to go on and not worry about what I have lost. I have decided to dwell on what I have."

That is the attitude we need. Instead of dwelling on past failures, we need to focus on upcoming challenges and victories.

The story of Jesus feeding the five thousand instructs us in this principle. When the boy gave Jesus two fish and five loaves, Jesus did not say, "My, my, what will I do? I have only two fish and five loaves to feed five thousand." Instead of giving attention to the problem, Jesus turned His attention to God and gave thanks (John 6:11).

God doesn't come to us asking, "What do you lack?" He asks exactly what Elisha asked, "What do you have?"

God takes whatever "something" we give Him and creates a solution.

A miracle is conceived the moment we shift our attention from what we don't have to what we have. A little boy ran through our church, rushed out the front door right by me and fell on the concrete walk outside, skinning his knee badly. He began to cry and scream, "My leg, oh my leg."

Picking up the little guy, I said, "Where has your eye gone?" Stunned, he stopped screaming and reached up to feel his eye. What happened? He shifted his attention from his skinned knee to his eye and stopped crying immediately.

When you feel as though you have nothing, exercise your faith. Consider this: faith is the *substance of things* hoped for and the *evidence of things* not yet seen. Faith is not what doesn't exist. Rather, faith is substance and evidence. Faith is *something.* Take your *something* to God, and He will create a solution to your problem.

That's precisely what happened with this widow. Her small amount of substance — a jar of oil — became what God used to create a miracle. What she thought to be of little use, God used mightily to create abundance in the midst of her need.

God uses what we offer in faith as the substance to create a miracle.

We can learn something very valuable here about ministry. If we are to minister to someone in need, that person may first have to talk at length about his or her problems. So listen. And after they give a vivid description of what they don't like, want or have, then ask, "What do you want? What do you need? And what do you have? What will you believe God for?"

Notice that the attention has shifted from the problems to the possibilities. When we started to build a new church, we sold our property downtown and received just enough money to buy seventy-five acres. All we had was a jar of oil. Our money purchased just the land — no building, no parking lot, nothing else.

By faith, we drew up plans for the building. By faith we dug a hole. By faith, we began to fill that hole with a foundation and then a building. All we had at the beginning was just a jar of oil and faith. But that was all the substance God needed to create a miracle. We discovered that money follows ministry. Do the ministry first, and God sends the money.

Are you facing an impossible problem? Is your church looking at an insurmountable mountain? Are you looking into the teeth of a terrible monster? Take whatever you have in faith to God. Tell the Lord what you have and what your heart desires by faith. Where your attention goes, the power flows. Let your attention shift from your problems to the source of power — Christ.

Factor #15
Where your attention goes, the power flows.

Ask yourself:

- Do you give your attention to problems or possibilities?
- Does the power flow to you from Christ, or do problems drain your strength and hope?
- What do you have that God can use?

Pray...

— to shift your attention from problems to God.

— to allow His power to solve your difficulties.

— to see what you have that God can use instead of complaining to God about what you lack.

FACTOR #16

Expect to Do Much With a Little

> Then he [Elijah] said, "Go, borrow thee vessels abroad of all thy neighbors, even empty vessels; borrow not a few" (2 Kin. 4:3).

There is a song that says, "Little is much when God is in it." In other words, expect God to take whatever is in your church, home and life and do much with it. People often ask me, "How do you motivate people?" What I know about motivation can be stated simply: I expect much from people.

I know that expecting much from people runs contrary to conventional wisdom. Conventional wisdom in our culture today seems to ask just the opposite. Many seem to believe that if we ask too much of others they will leave the church and go somewhere that expects little. Instead of seeking to go forward, we just try to maintain. Conventional wisdom teaches us to give little, pray little and do little. It offers the lie: If everyone will do just a little, a lot will be accomplished.

God's truth shatters the lies of conventional wisdom. The church can expect much because we know a God who can do much with whatever we have in the house. God does not ask, "What's the least you can do?" Rather, He demands, "What do you have?" In the story about the widow's oil, the widow gave all she had and then collected empty vessels. That reveals much. God needs us to surrender all so that He can use empty vessels for His purpose. When all the empty vessels had been used, the oil stopped flowing, and the miracles stopped. Many times we see fewer multiplication results in ministry because we have not given God all the available empty vessels.

Every person in your church can be an empty vessel. Beyond that, consider every person in your city as an empty vessel.

Constantly bring people to the Lord with whatever they have, urging them as empty vessels to expect Him to do great things.

Most of us have not yet begun to reach our potential in Christ. If ninety-year-old Brother Bore could lead a thousand people annually to the Lord, what about us? How many people does God desire to reach through each of us each year?

I believe one of the greatest sins that Christians commit is the sin of not reaching their potential in the Lord.

When we moved to our present church campus, we were considering how many seats we needed in our main building. I wanted to build it to seat 3,500 people. The church board and the people rose up and said, "7,000 is probably too little; let's build it for 10,000. Pastor, we've got to have a place for the people." They were seers. They saw in God's vision for us things that were not but claimed those things as though they were with the substance of faith. They were prepared to find many empty vessels for God to use. My people stretched my faith.

Recently we saw over one thousand people come forward on Thanksgiving to accept Christ. The altars overflowed, and we had to turn people away. I said to the congregation, "I wish I had listened to you and built this auditorium to seat ten thousand!"

We need others to encourage us to reach beyond what we have all that God has for us.

Give God whatever you have. It may seem that what you have is very little, especially compared to what others have. Nonetheless, give it to Him in faith, and He will work miracles. Expect Him to do much. Have great expectations. God works through positive expectations.

You can be certain that God doesn't give you dreams and visions to frustrate you. He never gives dreams and visions to humble you. His dreams and visions are given because you were made in His image and His likeness. You were meant to be a vessel for the activity of the Father on earth in time and space.

When my son, Matthew, was thirteen he said to me, "Dad, tomorrow's the big day."

I asked, "The big day? What are you talking about, tomorrow's the big day?"

He said, "Mom and I got this thing through the mail, and it said we've been chosen for the final sweepstakes drawing of $10 million dollars. Tomorrow is the drawing." Then Matthew added, "If we win, Dad, what are we going to do with it? Do we have to give it all to the church? Couldn't we keep $1 million dollars, Dad?"

"Sure," I said, "we'll keep a million of it."

Here is the point. Matthew had a vision, and he was willing to give what he had to God. You can become an empty vessel by giving all you have to God at a very early age. God does not care if you are young or old. He gave Abraham a big dream when he was seventy-five. God promised, "I'm going to make you a father of a multitude and a nation." Abraham expected God to do much with a little. He and Sarah were too old to have children — but they had one — because by faith they trusted the God of miracles.

Finally, in 2 Kings 4 we read that after the widow collected empty vessels, she went from Elisha and shut the door behind her. As her sons brought the vessels to her, she filled them all. That is what a pastor does in his church. A pastor pours the Word of God into his people until they become full and ready for ministry.

What are you expecting from God? Are you willing to give Him what you have and expect much in return? God is seeking empty vessels in His church into whom He can pour His Word, His Spirit and His power.

Factor #16
Expect to do much with a little.

Ask yourself:

- What little do you have? Will you give God what you have?
- Are you expecting much from God by faith?
- Will you become an empty vessel that He can fill and use for ministry?

Factor #16

Pray…

— to have great expectations in faith, trusting God to work mighty miracles with whatever you have.

— that your church will be filled with empty vessels whom God will fill and use.

— for the overflowing oil of the Holy Spirit to pour out of your life and into the lives of those around you.

MULTIPLICATION WITH BUSES

We have two bus ministries and over forty buses. On Sunday mornings, we bring children to church. On Sunday evenings, we bring adults.

Every Saturday our bus pastors go out to visit in the neighborhoods where they pick up people on Sunday. Every child that rides the bus is visited, whether or not he was in Sunday School the previous Sunday. The pastors also visit fifteen new homes to find children to take to church.

Some of the children we picked up years ago are now graduates of the Master's Commission.

On Sunday afternoons at 4:30 P.M., our adults go out of the buses for over two hours and round up people to come to church from the streets, government projects and apartment complexes.

On Sunday evenings we bring people from all of our Church on the Street ministries to share as a total community of Christians in worship.

An executive CEO went out to an Hispanic apartment building. He did not speak Spanish and came back with no one else on his bus. "I want to make this work," he told me, insisting on returning the next week. During the last three years that man has brought over one thousand people a year who have accepted Christ on Sunday night. Bus ministries will multiply disciples!

Factor #17

Write Your Vision Down

> I will stand on my guard post and station myself on the rampart; And I will keep watch to see what He will speak to me, and how I may reply when I am reproved. Then the Lord answered me and said, Record the vision and inscribe it on tablets, that the one who reads it may run (Hab. 2:1-2, NAS).

Some people would call this instruction from God, "Write down your goals." Others would label it as "creating a model," "forming a mold" or even "establishing a paradigm." Whatever your label, the command is simple: When God gives you a vision, *write it down!*

Why? If we want to do anything for God, we must clearly understand what His vision is for us. Without a vision, people perish (Prov. 29:18). And people are perishing. They are not living the abundant life that Jesus promised (John 10:10). Their potential in Christ has not been realized because they have not understood God's vision for them.

We must learn what it takes for a vision to be realized. Fundamental to realizing a vision is writing it down, inscribing it indelibly in our minds, hearts and actions. In other words, a vision is to be set in concrete or etched in stone. There must be resolve, determination, commitment and dedication. A vision must take form and be defined.

That happens only when it's written down for everyone to see and understand.

A construction worker would never pour concrete before having forms set in place in the shape the concrete must take. Likewise, we cannot ask for the power or substance of God if we have not yet set the forms of His vision within our hearts and our church. The substance of God's power must be poured into the clearly established form of His vision.

Explore with me how this works. A vision is like an outline for a speaker. There may be three, four or more points. To the outline the speaker adds substance — meat if you will — on each point. An outline becomes the mold into which the speaker pours the substance of his message.

A vision forms your life so that God can pour His substance, energy power and Spirit into you.

In just such a way, God's vision will take shape within you and be implemented in all you think, say and do.

All power in heaven and earth has been given to Christ who indwells us. Thus we have all power in Christ. We have the power to heal the sick, raise the dead, cast out devils and take our cities for God. "I can do all things through Christ who strengthens me" (Phil. 4:13). But that power must be channeled through the form of His vision which has been written down on the tablets of our lives. "Forasmuch as ye are manifestly declared to be the epistle of Christ ministered by us, *written* not with ink, but with the Spirit of the living God; not in tables of stone, but in fleshy tables of the heart" (2 Cor. 3:3, italics added).

Do you see it? Our lives are shaped by the form of His vision so that when He goes to write it down in our hearts, we become living letters to others about Christ.

When you receive a vision from God, write it down in your heart, thoughts and life. Never put God's vision on the shelf and forget it like a dusty book tucked away on some remote library shelf. Keep the vision ever before you. Write it down. Read it. Meditate upon it. Ponder it in your heart. Think about it continually. Why? It is the form, the outline and the vessel into which God pours His Spirit and substance.

After you write your vision down, fellowship daily with God about the dream. As you do, God reveals what is real about it and what is not. Jesus went up to the mountain to pray. He rose up early to pray, isolating Himself from the distractions around him in order to hear from His Father, who continually poured His vision into His Son's life.

I have written down God's vision for me and our church and continually commune with God about that dream. Now I find myself talking as if that vision is already in existence.

When you write down God's vision it begins to take substance.

For example, if God has given you a vision for a baby, then fix up a nursery in your home. Decorate it. Read every book you can about rearing children. Or, if you want to go into the ministry, begin to learn how to be a minister, preparing for the day that God opens the door.

MULTIPLICATION

Factor #17
Write your vision down.

Ask yourself:

- Do you know God's vision for your life and church?
- Have you written down that vision in your heart, thoughts and actions?
- Is your life so shaped and formed by His vision that you are ready to have His power and substance poured into you?

Pray...

— for God to write down His vision on your heart and in your thoughts.

— to be shaped by His vision, becoming the form into which He pours His substance and power.

Factor #18

Be Spilled to Be Filled

> And when they had prayed, the place was shaken where they were assembled together; and they were all filled with the Holy Ghost, and they spake the word of God with boldness (Acts 4:31).

Christians may differ in their theology about the baptism of the Holy Spirit. But regardless of our theology, all believers need to be filled with the Holy Spirit — continually, regularly and daily. Paul simply writes, "Be filled with the Spirit" (Eph. 5:18).

For the apostles, being filled with the Holy Spirit was not something that happened only once. It was an ongoing occurrence that always resulted in a demonstration of love and service to others.

Think about this: We have no need to be filled unless we have been poured out. And the more we are poured out, the more we need to be filled. Instead of asking one another, "Are you Spirit-filled?" we need to be asking, "Are you Spirit-spilled?"

The measure of our spirituality is not how much we receive but how much we give. It is how much of the Spirit and the grace of God flows through, not just to us.

I have heard people talk about how much they love a particular church because they really get blessed there. Getting blessed in church is important, but it is more important that you become a blessing, that you become someone else's miracle.

People argue about the biblical pattern of being filled with the Spirit, but if the biblical pattern tells us anything, it is that being filled with God's Spirit turns us into lovers and givers (1 John 4:12-13).

Every year at Christmas, I ask each person in our congregation to go out and buy a present for a hurting, underprivileged child in our city. The people can spend as much as they want, but the present has to be worth five dollars or more. I also ask them to pray that God will lead them to the present He wants them to buy.

Our people bring their presents and put them at the foot of our huge singing Christmas tree. Then we bring in over ten thousand underprivileged kids for a special Christmas program. One man gave one thousand new bicycles for these children. At the end of the service, we lead all the children into the auditorium.

The orchestra and the two hundred people standing on the forty-five-foot singing Christmas tree lead the congregation in the singing of carols as the children discover two mountains of presents under the tree, one for the boys and one for the girls.

Every year when those children come down the aisle, the adults in our congregation weep so much they can hardly sing.

Now please understand this: Even if it didn't bless any of those children, I would continue to give away presents for the sake of our congregation. Every person who puts a present under that tree has the opportunity to pour into an empty vessel. They have uncovered this truth:

The joy of being filled with the Holy Spirit comes from being spilled.

One year one of the little boys asked his bus pastor during the Christmas service to pray with him. "Do you think God would give me an electric train?" he asked.

The bus pastor really didn't know what to say as they prayed together. He was afraid that a disappointment could destroy the little boy's faith. He knew that someone in the church might have purchased a train. But the presents were wrapped and given out randomly. Nobody knew who would get what package. But God is faithful. Someone in the church had been led to buy a Lionel electric train set. And out of all that multitude of presents, that's the present the little boy received.

That young man will never forget that in the midst of eight thousand dirty, rambunctious little kids he was so special to God that his prayer was heard and answered.

His miracle was no less a blessing for the family that bought the present and the bus pastor who had the privilege of seeing the miracle happen as He poured into an empty vessel.

Factor #18
The more you're spilled, the more you are filled.

Ask yourself:

- Are you being filled continually with the Holy Spirit?

MULTIPLICATION

- How does He want to spill you today in order for you to be a blessing in the lives of others?

Pray...

— to be filled with the Holy Spirit.

— to be spilled and poured out as a blessing in the lives of others.

MULTIPLICATION INSPIRES GIVING

For years we have taught multiplication through our Pastors' School, sowing into the lives of many pastors and leaders and inspiring them to give.

Encouraging and equipping others to multiply and networking with churches inspires giving.

Pastor Charles Nieman started a bus ministry and gave hundreds of turkeys away on Thanksgiving. Over four hundred and sixty people were saved on one Sunday. He started taking monthly offerings for the Dream Center, sowing more than $85,000 into the Center, because, as he said: "Something good needs to come out of Los Angeles."

Willie George invested $1,000 in this ministry, then gave $50,000 more when the Queen of Angels hospital became available to us. After he visited the Dream Center, he felt led to give an additional $100,000 out of his building fund — a sacrifice of love and vision. His church is now multiplying as a result of their giving.

Sam Carr had a television station that was draining his church. He was about to give it all up when he heard the story of the ministry in Los Angeles and was so touched that he gave more than $33,000. A month later, a network bought his television station for more than four million dollars plus television time on the network.

Factor #19

Pentecost Is Possible Again

> And Jonathan said to the young man that bare his armor, Come, and let us go over into the garrison of these uncircumcised: it may be that the Lord will work for us: for there is no restraint to the Lord to save by many or by few" (1 Sam. 14:6).

God needs only a few people for Pentecost. For the first Pentecost, He needed only 120 people to save three thousand people in one day. And what God did yesterday, He can do again today.

For many years, John Wesley preached in England and witnessed thousands of people being saved. Then in 1784 he came to America and preached up and down the eastern seaboard. The greatest revival he preached during this time was in Augusta, Georgia.

Several decades later, an old country preacher was reading about the revival that Wesley had preached in Augusta. This African-American pastor determined to return to the exact spot of that great revival. For days he hitchhiked to Augusta. When he arrived, he found the church that Wesley had preached in and located the church's custodian. "Take me to the pulpit where John Wesley preached," he requested.

He was taken to the pulpit, and as he stood there he thought, *This is the pulpit from which John Wesley preached one of his greatest revivals.*

The elderly preacher asked the custodian to leave him alone. Then he got down on his knees, and with tears streaming down his cheeks, which were weathered and wrinkled from years of working in the fields, he prayed, "Lord, Lord, do it again, Lord. Do it again."

We are still waiting for God to do it again. The event described in Acts of one church seeing three thousand people saved in one day has never been repeated from the time of Pentecost two thousand years ago to today. But I believe Pentecost can happen again today. Why?

1. What God did yesterday, He can do today. God is able to perform any miracle again. If God healed the sick yesterday, He can heal today. If He saved three thousand yesterday in one church, He can do it again today. "For I am the Lord, I change not" (Mal. 3:6).

2. Just because it hasn't happened in two thousand years doesn't mean it can't happen. Human experience never dictates God's actions. Just because we haven't experienced something miraculous does not mean that God has stopped doing miracles. God can do it again. God reminds us in Isaiah 55:8 that His ways are not our ways.

3. When Pentecost does happen again, it will happen in the same way. Why? Because truth is truth in every age, in every situation and with every person. Jesus proclaims in John 14:12, "Verily, verily, I say unto you, he that believeth on me, the works that I do shall he do also." So if we are to have the same results or fruit that Jeus did, we must do the same works that He did.

4. Our Lord is a Lord of recipe. That means that God gave us a plan or a way to do things. He does not bless spontaneously without humans preparing for a blessing.

The early church gathered in Jerusalem in obedience to Christ. God responded with Pentecost.

5. God's plan always works when we work His plan according to His purpose. God's purpose and plan can be uncovered in Psalm 126:6, "He that goeth forth and weepeth, bearing precious seed, shall doubtless come again with rejoicing, bringing his sheaves with him." As we pray and weep for the lost while sowing the seed of God's Word into their lives, we will always bring in a harvest of saved souls.

6. God's plan includes people. God works through people. Pentecost was not something that God surprised His people with or caused to happen unexpectedly. Pentecost was a promised event that happened to and through people who allowed themselves to be used of God.

Pentecost was not accidental. Jesus trained his disciples for over three years. Jesus had a plan and a program to equip them. At times, we become irresponsible as preachers and leaders saying, "We don't need organization and programs. All we need is the Holy Ghost." But remember, God is an organized God. Jesus organized his disciples to feed the five thousand. He prepared seventy men to proclaim the gospel two by two. He appeared to five hundred witnesses after the resurrection. He had one hundred and twenty people praying and waiting for Pentecost in the upper room. Notice that numbers and counting are recorded throughout the Bible. Why?

God is a God of organization. He counts. He is concerned about numbers. He had Gideon number his army and Israel count the numbers in the tribes. He is a God of order and purpose with a plan for His church and all of creation.

God desires for us to walk in His purpose, to work His

plan and to get organized for the numbers of lost who will be saved.

Pentecost can happen again. But it is up to us to believe that it can; to pray and prepare for Pentecost; to be organized and ready to work God's plan. Where do we start?

- The people of Pentecost were saints like you and me. They had been sanctified, prepared and made available to God for whatever He wanted. Are you sanctified and available?
- They had organized and planned to be ready for Pentecost. Someone had a godly vision and said, "Let's gather together. Let's invite people to come. Let's pray in the upper room."
- They shared what God had done. They went out and told others what God had done in their lives after they had been filled with the Holy Spirit.

Pentecost didn't happen in that upper room only. If it had stayed there, we would not be Spirit-filled today. Rather, Pentecost happened when the apostles began to tell everyone. Are you ready for Pentecost to happen again?

Factor #19
Pentecost is possible again, because what God did yesterday He can do today.

Ask yourself:

- Do you believe that God will do today what He did yesterday at Pentecost?

- What are you doing to get ready? How are you organizing for a great outpouring of the Holy Spirit?

Pray...

— for Pentecost to happen again today.

— for readiness to be used by God in Pentecost today.

Factor #20

Want to Quit?

> Then I said, "I will not make mention of him, nor speak any more in his name. But his word was in mine heart as a burning fire shut up in my bones, and I was weary with forebearing, and I could not stay" (Jer. 20:9).

Yes, I have wanted to quit and undoubtedly, so have you. Anyone who has done anything for God has wanted to quit at one time or another. Having wanted to quit, I have learned some important things to share with pastors and leaders.

Wanting to quit is a sign of success. Why? Because successful people are the only ones who have the luxury of quitting. It's a good sign for you to want to quit, since it means that you actually have something to abandon.

I have more respect for the person who fails than for the one who never tried. Some time ago I drove by a housing project which had been abandoned. It had been started but never finished. Some of the foundations had been poured but never built upon. In the middle of the project were the charred remains of a house. I decided right then I would rather be the house that had burned than the one that was never built. For a moment, at least, the burned house had fulfilled the purpose for which it had been created. The house never built had no opportunity to be useful. Wanting to crash and burn is not all that disgraceful. In some ways, it is a sign of success.

The more you have to quit, the more tempting it is to quit. Let me explain. The higher you go, the more responsibility you have, the greater the call, the more frightening it becomes and the more tempting it is to quit. When God raises up a mighty leader, much is required of that person. It can be frightening to be in a high position of responsibility and visibility. When a mighty oak tree or redwood falls it takes far more with it than a tiny sapling.

I have the privilege to oversee a large and wonderful ministry with thousands of people involved each week. I guarantee you that I want to quit more than most. At times it feels overwhelming and scary to have so much to do. The temptation to quit intensifies as the ministry grows larger and larger.

You can enjoy the luxury of wanting to quit if you know that you're resolutely not going to quit. At a birthday party for me years ago my secretary of over twenty-three years commented, "One thing I can say about Pastor Barnett — he's no quitter." Yes, I may be a want-to-quitter, but I am not a quitter. Pay careful attention to this: Feeling like you want to quit at times is honorable. Quitting is not.

We have raised a generation of quitters. Little Johnny comes home with a poor report card, and his Mother says, "Poor Johnny, he is not very smart, but he sure is sweet." To comfort him about his "quitting" grades, Mother takes him out for an ice cream cone. Johnny strikes out playing baseball and wants to quit the team. Mother lets him quit, making excuses for him all the while.

Churches quit. They say, "It's not the day of revival. It's not the time for Pentecost, but the revival is coming."

They quit believing that God can act today by predicting that He will act some day in the future. Don't get me wrong. I am not looking down on those who have wanted to quit. I have wanted to quit all my life, but I haven't given up yet.

I wanted to quit cross country in high school, but I didn't. I wanted to quit the ministry as a young evangelist in West Texas and Kansas, but I didn't. I wanted to quit the first church I pastored in Davenport, Iowa, but I didn't. I wanted to quit when the *Republic* and the *Wall Street Journal* blasted me, but I didn't. Every Monday morning when the alarm goes off at 5:30 A.M. for prayer meeting, I want to quit, but I don't.

How To Keep From Quitting

What keeps me from quitting? What will keep you from quitting?

- Burn every bridge behind you so you can't go back and quit. In our church we have discovered that every miracle necessitates another miracle. There's nothing to go back for, so we move forward with God.
- Don't tell people you want to quit. Oh, you can share your feelings after God works a miracle in your life. I can tell others how I have felt in the past, but today's desire to quit is simply a momentary reaction not an eternal direction.
- Don't expose yourself to what you don't want to be. For example, people tell me they attend a church but don't really believe what that church believes. They

go there simply because they like the music, the pastor or a particular ministry. They are setting themselves up to quit. They are exposing themselves to an influence that tears down instead of builds up their faith.

- Lock yourself in so you cannot quit. Lock yourself in to God's vision, His Word and His purpose for your life so there will be no turning back. David sang, "My heart is fixed" (Ps. 57:7). Fix your heart on God, and you will never quit.

Why Can't We Quit?

Let me give you a few reasons why you and I can't quit.

1. God has said that he that puts his hand to the plow and looks back is not worthy of the kingdom (Luke 9:62).
2. We hold the future of this nation in our hands.
3. We are building faith and hope in our children.
4. There are lost cities that need the gospel.

I could list many reasons, but these are sufficient to make my point. Winners are people who persevere and do not quit. I often write on the reports my staff gives me about their ministries, "Great men are ordinary men that just wouldn't quit."

Factor #20
There's honor in wanting to quit — but don't!

Factor #20

Ask yourself:

- Are you feeling as though you need to quit?
- List five reasons not to quit and five people who are depending on you not to quit.
- What bridges do you need to burn so that you will not quit?
- Whose salvation is dependent upon your not quitting?

Pray...

— for strength not to quit.

— for people to encourage you.

— for the determination to finish what God has given you to do.

From the Streets to Bus Ministry

Leo's home was Skid Row in downtown Los Angeles. For weeks, Matthew invited him to come to the services on Thursday nights and to stay for the meal after the service.

When Matthew told me about Leo, I asked him why he was so persistent with this one man.

Matthew replied, "I keep believing the scripture that says, 'In due season you shall reap, if we faint not' (Gal. 6:9)."

One day Leo Pitts got on the bus and came to church. He accepted Christ, went through our discipleship program, and is now one of our head overseers for the entire campus. He goes back to the same place where he came from, takes people off the streets and disciples them in the Word of God. Leo also oversees a major portion of the bus ministry outreach.

Multiplication requires patience and persistence. On the streets we work with the same people, at the same locations, on the same days, for weeks and months at a time. Relationships have to be built. Love must be demonstrated. But if we are faithful, God will multiply the love and many just like Leo will be won to Jesus Christ.

Factor #21

Be an Entrepreneur for Christ

> For unto every one that hath shall be given, and he shall have abundance: but from him that hath not shall be taken away even that which he hath. And cast ye the unprofitable servant into outer darkness: there shall be weeping and gnashing of teeth (Matt. 25:29-30).

E*ntrepreneur* is a French military word that was once used to describe a particular type of commander who undertook risky ventures for strategic gains. Today the term has come to refer to business people who are action-oriented. They are not just thinkers. They are doers. Entrepreneurs can make a risky decision and act upon it. They have a passion for profit.

The parable of the talents tells the story of gospel entrepreneurs. Two of the servants, like entrepreneurs, were willing to risk great things with the talents that the master had given them. Out of great risk came great profit, and the master was pleased.

However, one servant had a "bunker" mentality. He hoarded his talent and buried it. As a result, no profit was made, and the master was displeased with this servant.

I see the church in this parable. Some churches become very entrepreneurial with the gospel. They are passionate for profit — souls saved for the kingdom. They are not content with only addition in evangelism. Such churches passionately desire multiplication — disciples being multiplied into the kingdom daily.

Churches that do not desire to be entrepreneurs for Christ develop a bunker mentality. They bury themselves behind programs, budgets, meetings and busy activities that happen behind closed doors. If someone happens to wander into their services and gets saved, then they are accepted into the fellowship. But there is no outreach, no risk, no passionate seeking for the lost to be saved.

In a best-selling book, *Target Success: How You Can Become a Successful Entrepreneur — Regardless of Your Background,* by Don Dwyer, certain characteristics of an entrepreneur are highlighted. The entrepreneur has:

- a value system.
- an orientation toward family.
- a strong work ethic.
- loyalty to country and those that bless him.
- spiritual faith.
- a caring attitude.
- inner happiness and contentment.
- a cautious attitude with his investments, investing wisely and not foolishly.
- management skills.
- the ability to communicate vision.
- a positive self-image.

Now these are the author's observations and not mine. But I do see some practical application of these qualities in light of Matthew 25.

Let me share with you what a church filled with entrepreneurs for Christ would look like as that church multiplies disciples for the kingdom of God. First, read Matthew 25:14-30 and then consider the following truths related to Christian entrepreneurs:

1. The Master chooses servants who will expand His kingdom.
2. The Lord invests in people instead of stuff.
3. The Master is willing to release control.
4. The Lord makes His servants accountable.
5. The Master is willing to take a risk.
6. The Lord gives resources for His servants to use not for them to hide.
7. Wise servants bring to the Lord an increase, and that pleases Him.
8. The increase also brings joy and great blessing to the servants.
9. A negative attitude toward God by a servant becomes the basis for misunderstanding in the kingdom.
10. Servants unwilling to invest are called wicked and lazy by God.
11. Servants who fail to use what the Lord gives them will lose it.
12. Servants who invest wisely will experience abundance in their lives.

God is looking for pastors, lay leaders and servants of all ages and backgrounds to become His entrepreneurs. He desires for us to risk everything, investing in the wisest investment of all — the saving of the lost. The profit from such investment multiplies and multiplies.

Think of the scores of people who will be saved because you and your church led them to Jesus.

Factor #21
Be an entrepreneur for Christ in spreading the gospel.

Ask yourself:

- Are you an entrepreneur for Jesus?
- Are you willing to take great risks with what He has given you to win the lost?
- How are you investing what Jesus has given you in the lives of others?
- In what ways does your church invest God's resources?

Pray...

— for wisdom in investing what God has given you.

— for passion to become an entrepreneur for Christ.

— for a church that takes risks to win people to Jesus.

FACTOR #22

Ask the Right Person

> You do not have because you do not ask (James 4:2).

These nine words contain the secret to poverty and powerlessness in the life of the church and the average Christian today.

So many pastors ask me, "Why do I see so little fruit in my ministry? Why doesn't my church grow? Why do the members help so little in the work of the church? Why do I grow so slowly in the likeness of Christ?"

Again God replies, "It is neglect in prayer. You have not because you ask not."

One day in Davenport, Iowa, I stood before my congregation and pleaded for workers and intercessors. I asked for people to commit themselves to becoming involved in winning the lost to Christ. I pleaded intensely and then asked for a show of hands. Very few people responded.

So I continued to berate my people. I chastised and rebuked them. I used the Bible to remind them that those who do not bear fruit will not grow and prosper and will even be cut down (John 15:6). Then I went home feeling blue, embarrassed and ashamed that I had yelled at my people in such an angry way.

As I sat in my living room feeling defeated, there was a knock on my front door. When I opened the door, a bubbly, Spirit-filled Baptist preacher, Scotty Thomas, who had been attending our church, bounded in and proclaimed, "I have been sent by God."

Scotty then proceeded to give me some godly wisdom. "Preacher, I love you. Good sermon tonight..." As he paused, I knew that after the buildup would come something piercing to my heart.

Then Scotty said, "You know we can do everything that we can do. We can work. We can challenge. But when we cannot get workers, there is only one way to find them. The Bible says we have to pray to the Lord of the harvest, and He will send workers" (Matt. 9:37-38).

That brief word changed my life.

We do not challenge, berate, chastise or motivate workers into the harvest. We pray them into the harvest.

One reason we have a multitude of harvest workers in Phoenix is that I and others have prayed literally for hours, "Lord, send the workers." If there are no workers for the harvest, examine the prayer life of the church.

In Acts 2:41 we read that the Lord added three thousand to the church. Then we skip over to Acts 5:14 and notice that by then multitudes were coming to the early church. At first addition increased the church, and then multiplication increased the church daily. How did they move from addition to multiplication? The answer is found in the intervening chapters of Acts — prayer!

Acts 2:42 observes that the early believers "continued steadfastly in the apostles' doctrine and fellowship, and in breaking of bread, and in prayers." Acts 4:31 reports, "And when they had prayed, the place was shaken where they were assembled together; and they were all filled with the Holy Ghost, and they spake the word of God with boldness."

Then in Acts 6:4 we read that they gave themselves to prayer. The early church was a praying church. As a result workers for the harvest were plentiful, healings abounded and signs and wonders followed them.

Why has our church in Phoenix continued to grow? Multiplication does not depend on great preaching, great buildings or great programs. It depends on great praying. Our church realizes that a mighty move of God will come only by prayer and fasting.

So the biggest difference between the church today and yesterday is that they lived in prayer while we wallow in prayerlessness. It seems that churches have a hard time even believing in prayer. We act as though management is more effective than prayer. E. M. Bounds commented that nothing is possible without prayer. Too often we pray to make ourselves feel better instead of praying until the place we assemble is shaken. When was the last time that your church was shaken by prayer?

If we really believed that prayer changes things, then every day we would pray for our children, for our nation and for new converts. We have not seen a harvest or workers for the harvest because we have not prayed and asked God.

We live amidst future shock. We rush into the future before we have fully lived the present. We seem to believe that our efforts, determination, confidence, methods and organization will accomplish whatever we desire.

Have we become so mesmerized by our own efforts that we no longer think that prayer really matters?

We act as though prayer is not really important and as though we have matured beyond the need to pray. In all of history, the church has never been so organized, computerized, specialized and equipped with surveys, data and statistics. Yes, all of these sources of information are wonderful, but if we are not careful, we will begin neglecting prayer and looking to our organization for power.

I believe the devil laughs at the church when we use our own schemes and devices to try to win the lost. He knows that no organization can ever defeat him. Only prayer will loose the chains of bondage and release the power of the gospel to a hurting world.

We have not because we ask not — we pray not. The power of God will be available for the harvest when we pray. Prayer releases personal holiness and hunger for God. It brings the power of God back into our work.

We need God's power to work in His harvest. The same power that raised Jesus from the dead is at work in us to raise others from the death of sin. Workers in the harvest are sent forth to raise the spiritually dead to new life in Christ. Only prayer can release workers filled with resurrection power. And the only reason we do not go forth in such power is that we ask not.

Factor #22
Multiplication depends on asking the right person.

Factor #22

Ask yourself:

- Are you praying for workers in the harvest?
- Is the place where you worship shaken by prayer?
- Are you experiencing His resurrection power through prayer?

Pray...

— for workers in the harvest.

— to become a worker in the harvest yourself.

— for your church to be shaken by the power of prayer.

RELEASE SUPERNATURAL FAITH

When supernatural faith fills the church, signs and wonders abound. Jesus told us that "prayer and fasting" will bring forth the supernatural (Mark 9:29).

The church needs seasons of prayer which offer every Christian a time to stay up all night in prayer and fasting.

When I was a child, an evangelist who came to my dad's church said to me, "Go home and be a miracle."

So I went home and prayed, "Lord, if I'm going to amount to anything, it will take a miracle."

Years later I returned to my dad's church as a young evangelist. I prayed and fasted before the meetings at his church. At the end of one service a mother brought her ten-year-old daughter with leukemia to me and said, "If you will pray for my daughter, I believe God will heal her."

I prayed for her, and then I went on my way. Later my parents called me. "Do you know what happened to that girl?" my mother exclaimed. "Her doctor examined her and found that all the cancer cells had disappeared. She is healed."

Years later the girl visited our church in Phoenix. She was a pastor's wife and living proof that prayer and fasting bring forth the supernatural power to heal.

Factor #23

Become a Miracle

> I can do all things through Christ who strengthens me (Phil. 4:13, NKJV).

In an effort to compliment me, a man once remarked, "Brother Barnett, you have literally performed miracles here."

Immediately, I responded, "No, no, no! I have not performed any kind of miracle, but I am a miracle."

I do not perform miracles, nor does any man. But we can become a miracle. The Bible declares that we are the workmanship of the Lord and were created for good works. If the church is going to multiply itself, then it will need to be filled with people who are miracles. So how does someone become a miracle?

Pray not for a task equal to your power, but for power equal to your task. God doesn't need your ability but your availability. Becoming a miracle does not depend on talent, charisma, ability or education. When your task gets bigger than you, you enter miracle territory. If you are equal to the task, then you do not need God or a miracle. However, when the task is bigger than you, God looks down and sees all that you must do and says, "Wow, there's an opportunity for a miracle."

Realize the task and strength never remain constant. Follow this closely. Your task will always require just a little bit more than your strength allows. Now, if you give up a task that God has given you, your present strength will diminish. If you want to be used of God, find and do every job He gives you to do. You will never grow until you are overworked.

Always start the task before you get the power. Consider powerlifting. A powerlifter gets strength only by lifting weights. The more powerlifters lift weights, the more strength they have. If they want to lift weights beyond their present capacity, they must start lifting before they receive the power to reach their goal. If they never start, they never attain their goal. So you don't get more strength *for* the work; you get strength *by* the work. For example, you don't get strength from God for praying. As you pray, you grow stronger. You do not receive strength for witnessing by talking about it. You get stronger as a witness for Christ by witnessing.

Our church is strong not because we have special events and pageants, not because we run buses, not because we have charisma, not because we have great facilities, but because our church has burdens that we cannot bear.

We have learned that when we have burdens we cannot bear and weights we cannot lift, the Lord reaches down and says, "I am going to help you bear your burdens because the task is bigger than you, and you left Me some miracle territory in which I can demonstrate My strength and show My glory."

We must always start the task before we get the power. Strength comes from God as we do the task. So I pray, "God, don't cut my work, increase it. If my task is larger, my strength will be larger and will increase. I want to grow, God. Make my burdens heavier so that I might see your miracle-working power."

Factor #23

Never pray to do miracles. Pray to be one. This is His work, not ours. We can never do all that we are supposed to do. That opens the door for a miracle.

Do you desire to be a miracle? Then tackle a task given by God even though you believe yourself to be incapable of the task.

Try something big. Reach for something beyond your grasp. Lift something greater than your strength. Step out and start by declaring, "I serve a God that will give the power." I am the work. He is the worker.

Factor #23
Become a miracle.

Ask yourself:

- Are you praying for miracles or praying to be a miracle?
- When will you step out in faith to do a spiritual task greater than yourself?
- What miracle does God want to do in and through you right now?

Pray...

— to be a miracle.

— not for strength but for a spiritual task to build your strength.

Factor #24

Qualify Yourself for a Miracle

> And thou shalt command the priests that bear the ark of the covenant, saying, When ye are come to the brink of the water of Jordan, ye shall stand still in Jordan (Josh. 3:8).

Before the people of Israel could possess the Promised Land they faced a problem — the Jordan River. A river blocked them from God's promise.

Most people regard problems as hindrances to miracles happening in their lives. Actually just the opposite is true. You cannot qualify for a miracle until you have a problem.

God was not satisfied with the Israelites staying in the wilderness. He wanted them to go a little further. First, they were to stand on the bank of the Jordan. Then, they had to stand in the Jordan. Finally, they would cross the barrier, the Jordan River, and enter the Promised Land. Only there they would find another problem — Jericho. But not to worry! The problem of Jericho would qualify them for another miracle.

Too often churches find themselves content with where they are when God wants them to go a little further. Our church has discovered that to experience miracles we must not be satisfied with today's blessings.

As a matter of fact, we are not satisfied with average. One enemy of the church is called *average.* Some churches must be above average in order to pull the below average churches up. Someone must be red hot to bring the temperature up in lukewarm and cold Christians.

There's always a problem out in front of us. There will always be a Jordan River, an obstacle and a barrier to what God wants us to do. Before we can see a miracle, we must go a little further.

I know many people that come to the edge of the river and say, "Nothing is happening. The water is not parting. I do not see God moving." So they back off and camp by the side of the river. They stand around studying the problem. Notice that the word "into" can be found in the text. It is when we go into the midst of the water, when we march headlong into the problem, that the waters part and the miracle is seen.

God's servants in Daniel would never have seen the fourth man in the furnace if they had not entered the furnace.

David would never have seen Goliath fall if he had not entered the battle.

Jesus would never have seen the resurrection if He had not faced the cross.

All of us want miracles. But there is a great risk involved in miracles. You have to step out into your problem, face your difficulties and confront your enemies before you will ever see a miracle.

What we want in churches is not miracles but magic. We seek God's miracles, but we don't want to experience any pain, struggle, effort or difficulties. However, there are conditions established by God for miracles. The first condition is to face the problem. Facing a problem calls for us to humble ourselves, pray, repent and seek God's face (2 Chr. 7:14).

Notice that each of these actions takes us a little further and a little deeper into God's power and presence. It's there — in His presence and power — that we find miracles.

For years I said from my pulpit that some day God was going to have someone give a million-dollar miracle. I am seeing God do a multi-million-dollar miracle in Los Angeles with the International Church.

Matt Crouch built and operates a television studio there, and his father, Paul, donated equipment for the studio valued at nearly $1 million dollars. Televangelists and other pastors donated tens of thousands of dollars. TBN gave us thirty minutes a week to share the vision of L.A. on television. Our Pastors' School pledged almost $700,000 to help us pay for the facilities. Then a guest visiting our church asked to see the ministry, and upon visiting it put a check in my hand. I counted the zeros. There were six of them. I had seen a million-dollar miracle happen not just once but many times over.

Do you know how I happened to see a miracle? The answer is simple. We kept going a little further into the water. We recognized problem after problem in Los Angeles, and God led us into the water. Once we entered the problems, God provided the miracles. Problems qualified us to see His miracles.

Factor #24
The one thing that qualifies you for a miracle is a problem.

Factor #24

Ask yourself:

- What problems am I now facing that block my miracles from God?
- Am I willing and is my church willing to face problems in order to see God's miracles?

Pray...

— for the willingness to face and enter into your problems.

— for humility and the desire to repent, pray and seek God's face for your problems.

— for a church willing to step into problems in order to qualify for God's miracles.

INVESTING IN GOD'S KINGDOM

A friend of mine for over forty years invited me to the classy, black-tie banquet where he was to be inducted into the Automobile Hall of Fame in Detroit, Michigan.

Michael Cardone, a Spirit-filled Christian, was dying of cancer the evening he stood to receive his award. He had been coughing so hard during the day that we all doubted he could speak. But he gave a profound testimony in front of many who did not know Jesus.

Michael Cardone invested his resources and talents in God's kingdom for years. He gave money to Oral Roberts University for a building to educate young Christians. In Springfield, Missouri, he gave funds for a Christian media center and a new theological school building.

Michael Cardone had lived life as a Christian entrepreneur. Even fighting a terminal disease, he looked forward to ways he could serve Christ. As he finished his speech, he said, "We have only just begun." Now his son, Michael Cardone, Jr., is seeing his business multiply as a result of his father's investment in the kingdom.

He knew that you don't hold on to what you have. You take a risk for the sake of the gospel.

In risking all for the kingdom, he experienced the greatest profit — an abundant life in Christ Jesus.

Factor #25

Build a Risk-Taking Church

> By faith Noah, being warned of God of things not seen as yet, moved with fear, prepared an ark to the saving of his house; by which he condemned the world, and became heir of the righteousness which is by faith (Heb. 11:7).

Every church is living in one of three stages: risk-taking, caretaking or undertaking. Most churches begin their existence as risk-taking churches because they are usually planted or birthed in the midst of revival or renewal.

Noah models this risk-taking lifestyle. For 120 years he built an ark in preparation for something he had never experienced — rain and floods. By faith he took a risk and suffered the world's ridicule and laughter.

Everyone talks about walking by faith, but too many desire a fail-safe faith. They want their walk to be risk-free. However, faith is a life in which we put everything on the line for Christ.

Many desire to move in God and to exercise their spiritual gifts. They want to be used by God. So they attend classes, seminars, conferences and even enroll in our Master's Commission program or a Bible school. But too often their ultimate goal is not how to *take* risks but how to minister *without* risk.

Risk-taking Christians and churches are always on the

cutting edge of ministry and life. They boldly march into God's future. Their focus is on God's dream and vision for tomorrow. The best is always yet to come. Risk-taking churches invest all they are today in Christ to become all they can be in Christ tomorrow.

A caretaking church carefully plans for the present. They are not oriented toward the future. Caretakers basically try to care for themselves today, carefully planning for the present hour.

Undertaking churches are always looking back. They continually tell stories about yesterday when the church was great. They speak of past revivals and great events that the church has experienced. They fondly remember how God shook the church yesterday.

Each stage has its own theme song. The undertaking church sings, "When the roll is called up yonder, I'll be there." The caretaking church intones, "Hold the fort for I am coming." But the risk-taking church triumphantly marches to refrains of, "Onward, Christian soldiers, marching as to war...like a mighty army moves the church of God."

Risk-takers expectantly proclaim, "God is doing a new thing." Caretakers cautiously declare, "I hope nothing unusual happens today." Undertakers just look around and say, "What happened?"

Remember this:

God is the greatest risk-taker of all.

He risked having His son die on the cross for those who would accept His sacrifice of love. Jesus risked spreading the gospel with twelve disciples. He had no back-up plan.

The church that takes risks walks by faith and not by sight (2 Cor. 5:7). What qualities does such a church possess? Here's a checklist for you:

✔ The church is oriented to the future not to the past.
✔ People are more important than policy.
✔ Organization springs out of God's vision not out of management strategies.
✔ Dreams dictate direction.
✔ Seeking to be fail-safe is replaced by being risk-takers who trust God.
✔ Members are dependent on God instead of man as their source. Their security is in God alone.
✔ Instead of following good ideas, members pray for and follow after God's ideas.

Build a risk-taking church for Jesus Christ.

Factor #25
Build a risk-taking church.

Ask yourself:

- Are you relying on God as your source?
- Will you risk everything on His dream and vision for you and your church?
- Do you walk by faith and not by sight?

MULTIPLICATION

Pray...

— that your church becomes a risk-taking church.

— that you will seek God's dream and vision.

— for God's ideas for your future.

Factor #26

Enlarge Your Circle of Love

> Be kindly affectioned one to another with brotherly love; in honor preferring one another; not slothful in business; fervent in spirit; serving the Lord; rejoicing in hope; patient in tribulation; continuing instant in prayer; distributing to the necessity of saints; given to hospitality (Rom. 12:10).

We must become aware of our tendency to draw circles. What do I mean? People tend to draw circles around people who are acceptable to them and exclude people from their circles who are unacceptable.

Having the mind of Christ means that our circles should exclude no one and include everyone. Paul writes, "Wherefore receive [accept] ye one another, as Christ also received [accepted] us to the glory of God" (Rom. 15:7).

I have to be very careful in my hatred of sin not to hate the sinner. It is possible to love the sinner and hate the sin. If the church today is to truly express Christ's love, then we cannot exclude anyone.

Does your circle include those who have wronged you? Does your circle include those who backbite and hurt you? Isn't it interesting that Jesus' circle of intimate friends included Judas? Can your circle include a Judas within it? If so, you will receive healing, restoration and blessing. You will never know the full blessing God has for you, your church and your ministry until your circle includes all those that God includes.

Here are some important revelations:

- The only one who can hurt or wound you is the one excluded from your circle.

One reason the church is not fulfilling its mission is that too many people have been excluded. We think the church is a waiting room for saints. However, the church is a hospital for the sick. The attitude of the average church seems to be: "Don't let them in because they will corrupt the church." The moment our church in Phoenix let me in as the pastor, the church was corrupted. The truth is that all of us are sinners redeemed by the blood of Christ. We are a part of His circle of love not because we are acceptable but because we are accepted. Once you exclude someone, you make that person your enemy.

- Church membership is based on God's acceptance not on human qualifications.

One philosophy of church membership holds that not just anybody can join a church. A candidate for membership must vow that he or she will do or not do certain things before the person will be accepted. The other philosophy of membership states that if God accepts them, they can join. We'll take them as they are and help them grow in grace. We'll accept them into our circle of love, and they will mature in Christ along with us. Legalism is very narrow and exclusive. But love is inclusive of all whom God accepts.

- Our circle of love must include the thing about which we feel most ashamed.

We feel shame when we feel separated from friends and from God. Everyone in a church has something shameful in his past. If we include in our circle that which is shameful, God will cover it with His forgiveness, glory, beauty and loveliness. If we are to have boldness and confidence in the church, we have to release our shame. Release begins when we include it in our circle of love.

We include in our circle of love the most shameful symbol in history — the cross. On the cross, Jesus became sin and shame for us. We include shame in our circle of love.

What people are you seeking to exclude from your church? Who is so bad and shameful that you cannot love him or her? Are homosexuals, perverts, thieves, abortionists or murderers excluded? Who is on your exclusion list?

Once you have identified whom you exclude, you will have an important mirror for looking at yourself. Whom we exclude tells us more about ourselves than about the excluded. Our fears, sins, insecurities and prejudices are revealed by those we choose to exclude.

If there is anyone that you or your church need to include in your circle of love, do it now. Including them will transform both them and you.

Factor #26
Enlarge your circle of love.

Ask yourself:

- Do I or my church exclude certain people or groups

from our circle of love?

- How will I enlarge my circle of love?
- Whom do I exclude? What does that reveal about myself?

Pray...

— for Christ to empower you to accept others.

— for the boldness to enlarge your circle of love.

Purpose Motivated by Love

I watched as some retarded children lined up to run the hundred-yard dash in a Special Olympics. As the starter's gun sounded, they sprinted down the track, each child straining every muscle to win the race.

One child pulled out in front of the rest. Suddenly the runner a few steps behind the leader stumbled and fell to the ground. The first place runner stopped dead in his tracks, went back to the fallen runner and helped him to his feet asking, "Are you OK?" Then the one who had been in the lead helped his friend across the finish line.

As I watched this scene unfold, I thought, *Who is retarded after all?*

Too often we who call ourselves "normal" are actually retarded in our ability to love others.

We can learn from this example. Yes, the purpose of the race was to cross the finish line. But the motivation behind that purpose was love. Multiplication happens when unselfish people are motivated by love.

Jesus reminded us that in His kingdom, the first will be last and the last first. So pick up that person next to you and carry him to the finish line for the sake of God's glory.

FACTOR #27

Motivate Through Relationships

> Feed the flock of God which is among you, taking the oversight thereof, not by constraint, but willingly; not for filthy lucre, but of a ready mind; neither as being lords over God's heritage, but being examples to the flock (1 Pet. 5:2).

I am often asked the question, "You seem to have a very close relationship with your congregation. How can you be so close to so many people?" I do not understand fully how this intimate relationship happens, but I personally feel that every person I meet is special, unique and a miracle. I genuinely love the people in our congregation. I do know that if the relationship is not right between pastor and people, then a church will never be motivated to win souls and serve Jesus Christ.

How does a right relationship of intimacy between pastor and people become a reality? I do not have all the answers, but here are some ideas that have worked in our congregation. I believe the pastor sets the stage for such a relationship. So to pastors I would say:

1. Express your love openly. After I preach on Sundays, I stand at the door and shake hands with and hug everyone that I can. I love them, brag on them and encourage them.

2. Listen to your critics. You don't have to do all that your critics suggest, but do listen to them.

3. Do not strike the second blow. Refuse to retaliate. I have noticed in football games that the one who strikes second often gets penalized even though he didn't start the conflict.

4. Be quick to apologize. I try, and sometimes I fail. So I have learned how to apologize for my mistakes.

5. Never show your anger publicly. The Bible advises us in Ephesians 4:26, "Be ye angry, and sin not." Publicly berating someone never heals and always hurts.

6. Reward faithfulness openly. Affirm others. Honor and thank God publicly for what others do in ministry.

7. Give others credit and accept none. Of course, we never accept any of God's glory. But it is appropriate to honor others when they have worked hard, faithfully serving the Lord. Every Sunday I like to recognize the nursery workers. They deserve great credit for the ministry they do which allows parents to worship God and be involved in ministry.

8. Heal the hurt when someone is wounded. I never take Monday off because it is the day I gather up all the hurts that may have been caused on Sunday and seek to heal them.

9. Walk slowly through the crowd. Years ago I caught myself shaking hands with one person while looking past that person to the next in an earnest attempt to see everyone. As a result, I missed giving my attention to the one right in front of me. Now I give each person I encounter my attention and look them in the eye.

10. Let others save face. A businessman once said to me, "Sometimes a relationship is more important than being right." A relationship *is* more important than being right, winning an argument or proving a point.

11. Always befriend the little person. Those that seem insignificant and unimportant — be their friend.

12. Make all the friends you can on the way up because you may need them on the way down. When you are in a position to give, do so. There will come a day when you need to receive, and those that have received from you in the past will minister to your need.

13. Keep all the cards on the table. When people know that you are transparent, they will trust you. Remember, you have nothing to fear, nothing to hide and nothing to lose. The love of Christ has conquered your fear. When you confess your sins, you come clean and are forgiven. And since you have lost your life in Christ and know that everything belongs to him, no one can take anything from you.

14. Lead by example. Paul said to follow his example. If chairs need to be put up after a service, be right in the middle helping your people.

15. Be predictable. Let your people know what to expect of you. Don't preach on money when you've told your people to bring the unsaved. Keep a schedule so people know where you are and how to contact you.

16. Believe in people. Expect that your people will do something great for God.

17. Be transparent and vulnerable. Let people know that you are human and have real feelings and a real life.

18. Have a certain mystique about you. People do not need to know and understand everything about you. Mystique happens when a pastor spends time alone with God, getting to know His will and hearing His voice.

19. Be able to identify with your people. Understand what your people are going through and the demands upon their lives.

A leader must be able to relate to his people, to love them and to care for them. Love covers a multitude of sins — especially in a pastor's life! Amen.

Factor #27
An intimate relationship with the pastor motivates a church.

Ask yourself:

- As a pastor, am I building an intimate relationship with my people? As a lay person, do I have a caring and loving relationship with my pastor?
- Which of the qualities listed needs to be worked on the most in my church?

Pray...

— for the pastor and people in your congregation to develop a loving, caring relationship.

FACTOR #28

Overcome Excuses

> Ye shall be witnesses unto me both in Jerusalem, and in all Judea, and in Samaria, and unto the uttermost part of the earth (Acts 1:8).

There are several reasons why people do not win souls. Years ago I found out how difficult it is to get people to come out and do church visitation and evangelism, so I am sharing with you some reasons people give for not becoming soul-winners and some means to overcome these hindrances.

1. People do not win souls because they don't know how.

Churches often expect people to witness but do not equip their members to witness. Inspiration without education leads to frustration. We need to train people to be soul-winners. In Phoenix we have developed the *Saturday Soul-winning Society.* This is a simple thirteen-week course designed to equip people to lead others to Christ. You need to be equipped if you have not been. Your church needs such a course if it does not have one. How to obtain more information about this course can be found at the end of this book.

2. People do not win souls because they are afraid.

Fear of rejection or of appearing foolish often hinders people from witnessing. The fear of knocking on an unknown door and asking, "Do you know if you would go to heaven if you died today?" simply paralyzes some folks.

3. People do not win souls because they have not set a time in their schedule to witness.

Everyone must have a schedule with a time slot set aside for witnessing. You may say, "From two until five o'clock every Saturday afternoon I am going out soul-winning."

We worked together in my first congregation to overcome these obstacles to soul-winning.

I said to the church, "How many of you would win souls if you were trained and could overcome your fear? How many would come for one hour on Saturday mornings for thirteen weeks to be trained?" More than 250 signed a contract to be faithful each week, work with their leaders and pray and fast for power. After thirteen weeks, 267 people graduated and started going out to witness during a set time each week. That group of people led over fifteen hundred people to Jesus Christ. I have been setting up Saturday Soul-winning Societies ever since. The course materials are used all over the world. The course we recommend may be the most-used soul-winning course available today.

In the process of training, we give people biblical reasons why they must win souls and why they cannot remain silent about the gospel. I am sharing those reasons with you so that you will be motivated to get trained if you are not already a soul-winner, and you will have these reasons to share with others.

MULTIPLICATION

Five Reasons Why I Must Win Souls

1. Soul-winners are wise (Prov. 11:30).
2. Soul-winners are partners with the Lord (2 Cor. 6:1).
3. Soul-winners will shine (Dan. 12:3).
4. Soul-winners are happy (Ps. 126:5-6).
5. Soul-winning covers a multitude of sins (James 5:19-20).

Four Reasons Why I Cannot Remain Silent About Jesus

1. Jesus commanded all Christians to go and make disciples (Matt. 28:19-20).
2. Jesus' love for His people and their love for Him compels Christians to be soul-winners (John 14:15,21).
3. People of the world will perish without Jesus Christ (Rom. 6:23).
4. God is not willing that any should perish (1 Tim. 2:4; 2 Pet. 3:9).

I want to encourage and urge you to become a soul-winner. If you are fearful, work beside someone who has confidence in the Lord and is a bold witness. Learn from him. Be trained and equipped. And begin today to pray for the lost.

Factor #28
Overcome the reasons people have for not being soul-winners.

Ask yourself:

- Am I willing to be trained and equipped as a soul-winner or to be a trainer for others?
- Have I set aside a time to lead others to Jesus each week?

Pray...

— to become a soul-winner and to train and encourage others to be soul-winners.

MINISTERING TO COUPLES

About five years ago, Pastor Leo, a pastor on our staff who had over four hundred couples in his young couples' Sunday school class, said to me, "No one speaks nationally for the Spirit-filled community about marriage."

Needing to be proven in ministry as builders of strong marriages before we went national with a ministry, we multiplied ministry to couples with a strong Sunday School class as a foundation for ministry. God restored marriages miraculously. We virtually eliminated divorce among our church members in a city with a very high divorce rate.

God gave us the vision to create an annual conference to network with other churches that desired to equip leaders and minister to married couples. We have seen a revival in marriages. We have a worship team comprised of formerly divorced and now remarried couples and a discipling ministry that helps couples learn how to prevent conflict and divorce.

One of our largest resources for birthing people into ministry is our couples' ministry.

Most of our Sunday School teachers and workers come through this ministry.

Strong marriages definitely help a church multiply disciples throughout the congregation and community.

FACTOR #29

Reach for Your Potential in Christ

> By the rivers of Babylon, there we sat down, yea, we wept, when we remembered Zion. We hung our harps upon the willows in the midst thereof. For there they that carried us away captive required of us a song; and they that wasted us required of us mirth, saying, Sing us one of the songs of Zion. How shall we sing the Lord's song in a strange land? (Ps. 137:1-4).

The psalmist laments the lost potential and greatness of Israel. He mourns about how Israel used to be free, powerful and mighty in the Lord. In the past there was a song to sing, but now God's people have no song. All their potential had been wasted in sin and idolatry.

All over America there are churches mourning their lost potential. Some had revival in the past. Others were large but now their numbers are a fraction of former multitudes. Failing to reach their potential in Christ, some churches are contemplating shutting their doors.

The saddest people and churches in the world are those to whom God gave a plan that they failed to implement for God. God laid something before them, and they refused to grasp His plan and purpose. Potential requires commitment, sacrifice and work. How sad when a church turns from its potential, believing the price to be too high and the sacrifice too great.

God's potential will come to a person or a church as a gift. With potential, God gives *plan, promise and power.*

The plan and the promise always come before the power. For some, that presents a difficulty. They want the power first. We never see God giving power to people who decide to pull up short of their potential. So how does God want us to claim our full potential in Christ?

God wants a church that looks for hurt.

God desires churches to be on an expedition to find need. We saw a need for ministry to those in wheelchairs. We went on an expedition to find and buy wheelchair buses. Find a need and meet it. Out of the need to minister to those in wheelchairs came a plan from God, and His promise to provide the resources to meet that need. Then came the power to implement the plan and to build an entire ministry for the handicapped.

God wants a mobilizing church.

He wants a church that makes disciples and sends them around the world to make more disciples. We do not have a church that merely puts up a sign saying, "All visitors welcome." We go into the hedges and highways compelling people to come.

God wants a modeling church.

This church will be a pattern and example of good works. We want the world to see the light of Jesus shining through us.

What attacks the church's potential? Division. And who causes division? Those who major in minors; those who make essential the nonessentials; those who strain to see a speck of sin in others while missing the mountain of sin in their own lives; those more concerned with style than substance; and those who divide and split the church. Division spills out of the glue of disunity and sticks us to worldly concerns when our focus should be on godly potential.

In the book of Acts we see that the church realized its God-given potential because it moved ahead in "one accord," in unity.

Factor #29
Reach for your potential in Christ Jesus.

Ask yourself:

- Am I a unifying factor in my church which can enable us to realize our potential in Christ?
- Will I stop nit-picking in the church and begin to model Christ in all that I do and say?

Pray...

— to realize God's potential in your life and in your church.

— for unity in the body of Christ so that the world can see our good works and glorify God.

FACTOR #30

Be Better Than Average

> And ye have heard it was said by them of old-time, Thou shalt not kill; and whosoever shall kill shall be in danger of the judgment: But I say unto you, That whosoever is angry with his brother without a cause shall be in danger of the judgment (Matt. 5:21-22).

What contribution are you or your church making that will last for eternity? As I grow older, I wonder at times if the world will be a better place because I have passed through it. What about your life? Do you stand above the crowd? This text from Matthew points to a spiritual principle — go beyond what's required, and be better than average. Go beyond murdering — don't hate. Go beyond stealing — don't covet. Go beyond committing adultery — don't lust.

Christians have been caught in the trap of average and stuck in the rut of mediocrity by comparing ourselves to others instead of to Christ. Too often church leaders compare their church to others in their town or denomination. They mistakenly believe that if they are doing better than most then God must be pleased. However, our only standard for comparison should be Christ himself (2 Cor. 10:12-13).

Let me share three observations that show why being average is sinful and how to be better than average:

1. Those who are average fellowship with failure.

In order to maintain average, at times we rise above average but at others times we fall below average into failure. God does not want His people or His church to fail. I do not associate with failure. Jesus taught that loving only those who love us makes us average but that loving our enemies puts us above average.

Jesus hates average. He wants us to rise far above the world's standards. Jesus never said that He had come that we might just survive. Rather, He came that we might have abundant life (John 10:10). God desires that we go beyond surviving and prosper in all that we do (3 John 2).

2. It will take above average people to raise our world from where it is to where God wants it to be.

The church rises above the average so that the world can see a higher standard of morality, caring and service. The world will beat a path to the above average church that is prepared to meet the needs of an average world.

We set the standard for righteousness, purity and compassion. How sad it is when churches have as high a divorce rate as the world. The fact that everyone else is "doing it" does not excuse us. We must rise above the average in our homes, marriages and relationships. Let's raise the standard for the world to live up to instead of coming down to the world's ways.

The church should be better than the world in the way it treats people who work in it. The church must offer better "customer service" than the world. The church is called to live with higher financial, moral and ethical standards than the world's average. Instead of the church copying the world's new ideas, let the world start copying the church. Let creativity, innovation, new ideas and excellence begin in the church.

3. We make our world worse by being average because there is no one left to counteract all that is below average.

I believe that God's people can do better than the world's average. More is expected of us than of the world, not because we are better, but because our standard is higher.

Our example rises far above the world's average. Christ is the standard which lifts us up above average.

More is expected of we who are His church.

God expects more of us because He has empowered us with His Holy Spirit. He has filled us with the love of His Son. He has defeated sin and death on the cross and given us the good news to take to the world. In this age we have more wealth, more media to communicate the gospel, more facilities, more Christian education, more resources and more people to take the gospel to the world than ever in history. To whom much is given, much is required (Luke 12:48).

We have over two hundred ministries to reach out to the lost and hurting in our church and community. We are one of the largest congregations not only in our nation but in our world. Nonetheless, what has been accomplished is not the standard for another church. The churches in the world that are larger than ours will never be our standard of comparison. We have only one standard — Jesus

Christ. He has said to us, "More is expected." And He will continue to lift us up above what is average and to challenge us beyond our best until that day when He returns.

Factor #30
It's a sin for the church to be mediocre — so be better than average.

Ask yourself:

- Am I content with my Christian life? Am I making a difference?
- Do I rise above the average? Is the world a better place because of my Christian commitment? Do I stand among the faithful, brave and true? Do the lost see Christ in me?

Pray...

— for courage to live above the average and beyond your best.

— for the Holy Spirit to empower you to change your world for Christ.

BLESSED TO BE A BLESSING

Eugene Reisner was trying to start an inner-city church in Houston with no building and eight people who met for services under an overpass bridge. After attending our first Pastors' School in Los Angeles where I took up an offering for the Dream Center, Eugene decided to give $2,500 of the $3,300 his church had accumulated in a building fund for a church building.

Later, Eugene found a building that cost $250,000. The owner asked for $25,000 in down payment. His heart broke as he started to walk out of the building. As he got to the door, with tears in his eyes the owner said, "I'm not a believer. I don't know why I'm doing this but I am going to give you this building."

A church in Houston gave them a dormitory, a church building and $90,000 for their ministry.

Multiplying ministries inspire people to give, and they, in turn, receive multiplied blessings.

By sowing into a ministry greater than his, Eugene Reisner experienced God's multiplication in his own ministry. God multiplied facilities and people in a way greater than he ever imagined.

FACTOR #31

Rebound to Do Something Great

> That they may recover [rebound] themselves out of the snare of the devil, who are taken captive by him at his will (2 Tim. 2:26).

One of the most important aspects of the game of basketball is rebounding. If someone misses a shot, the most important thing to do is crash the boards and get the rebound. The same principle applies in the church. Everyone misses the mark at times. So the importance of rebounding in the church cannot be overstated. How well do you rebound the missed shots?

The Bible is filled with stories about heroes who were rebounders. Moses rebounded to serve God after he murdered an Egyptian. Rahab rebounded to an honored place in the genealogy of Jesus after she had been a prostitute. Ruth rebounded to marry Boaz after the death of her husband. David rebounded to become Israel's greatest king after sinning with Bathsheba. Peter rebounded to become a great apostle after denying Christ three times. And Paul rebounded to become history's greatest missionary after persecuting and killing Christians.

The list is much too long for us to rehearse all the names. But what about you or your church? You may have been fired as the pastor of a church or removed as a volunteer. You may have attempted a unique ministry only to see it crumble and disappear into oblivion.

You may have tried to lead someone you care about to Jesus but that person rejected both you and Christ. You may be down, but you are not out. The Holy Spirit within gives you the power to rebound.

Great men and women of God are ordinary people that will not quit. They just keep rebounding. They keep coming back. They keep on receiving God's forgiveness and sharing it with others.

The greatest symbol of rebounding is not a basketball backboard or even the story of a great rebounder. The cross is the greatest symbol of rebounding. Jesus appeared to be completely defeated. His disciples had abandoned Him. The religious and political leaders of that day rejected Him. The crowds that had followed Him all melted away. And Jesus died an ignominious death, on a cross, despised and rejected by humanity. Yet He rebounded. On the third day, God raised Him from the dead.

There is no failure too great and no sin too terrible for God to forgive. You can rebound — Christ did. The same power that allowed Him to rebound is now available to you through the Holy Spirit.

Factor #31
A secret of doing something great for God is rebounding.

Ask yourself:

- Have I given up? Is my church defeated?
- Will I claim Jesus' resurrection power to rebound?
- Who needs the witness of my rebound in order to be saved?

Factor #31

Pray...

— to see beyond every failure to the concrete hope of rebounding in Christ.

— for opportunities to encourage others to rebound in Christ.

Factor #32

Start a Saturday Soul-Winning Society

> How then shall they call on him in whom they have not believed? and how shall they believe in him of whom they have not heard? and how shall they hear without a preacher? and how shall they preach, except they be sent? as it is written, How beautiful are the feet of them that preach the gospel of peace, and bring glad tidings of good things!" (Rom. 10:14-15).

Every Christian is called to be a soul-winner, to go into his or her world and share the gospel of Christ with the lost. One of the most effective ways of "going" is to send equipped Christians into your city. A church without effective visitation of the lost will never begin to multiply disciples.

How does effective visitation help to win the lost to Christ? We asked deacons and deaconesses to become actively involved in soul-winning. Let me list the guidelines for visiting the lost that we give to them.

1. Establish a definite time to visit the lost. Guard that time carefully. As the time approaches, distractions and attacks from the enemy will fill your life. But no matter what time is set, stick to it with concrete resolve. Saturday morning is an excellent time for visitation.

2. Be soul conscious. Remember that the purpose of the visit is to lift up Jesus Christ. I do not care if a home is filled with religious slogans and pictures. It does not matter if the people visited are listening to Christian television or display Christian stickers on their car. Find a time to ask, "Are you a Christian? Do you know Jesus Christ as your personal Lord and Savior?"

3. Be neat and clean. Do not let your personal appearance or dress distract another person from Christ. Look good and smell good. Your personal appearance is important when you witness.

4. Carry a New Testament with you. Do not carry your fifteen-pound study Bible. That can be intimidating. Have your New Testament in a pocket or purse where you can reach for it easily.

5.Go two by two. Jesus sent out His disciples two by two. One encourages the other. Don't go alone.

6. Let one person do the talking. It becomes confusing when both people try to talk at the same time. While one talks, let the other person pray and observe.

7. Go with different people. Train others to win souls. Allow other people to do the talking, and then review with one another what happened during the visit after you leave the home. Learn from one another.

8. Pray for the filling and anointing of the Holy Spirit before going. The Holy Spirit will give you the words you need to say. Pray with your partner before your visits.

9. Go believing. Have a positive attitude. Believe that the Holy Spirit will lead the people you visit to Christ.

10. Be kind. That's a biblical commandment (Eph. 4:32). Be careful about the use of religious language. Do not say constantly, "Praise the Lord" or "Hallelujah, brother." Always be courteous and never argue with the people you are visiting.

11. Be accepting and affirming. Look for ways to affirm and compliment the people you visit.

12. Be careful about going inside. Those you are visiting may not want you in their home. Their house may be a mess. Remember that they may not know you. You can visit on the front porch if necessary.

13. Be a good listener. Listening is one of the greatest gifts you can give to another person. Listening affirms others and shows them honor and respect. Listening gives you insights into their needs and thus a way to apply the gospel to those needs.

14. When you get into a soul-winning dialogue, stay on the subject. Focus on salvation not on controversial doctrines. Do not be critical of other religions or church groups. Focus on Jesus Christ. If you do not know the answer to something, admit it and promise to find the answer.

15. Help them get lost. Now that may sound paradoxical. However, until a person knows they are lost, they will not know they need to be found, to be saved.

16. Keep the message simple. We like to use the Four Spiritual Laws by Bill Bright. Others prefer to use the Roman Road. Still others like to introduce Jesus through the gospel of John. Know how to present Jesus, and keep it simple. A simple progression of scriptures for salvation is found in Romans (3:23; 6:23; 5:8; 10:13).

17. Always ask the unsaved to receive Jesus. Ask them if they would go to heaven if they died. Explain to them the wages of sin and point them to the cross of Jesus Christ. When they receive Christ, ask them to pray with you, repenting of sin and receiving Jesus.

18. Invite them to church. Sit with them in church.

Walk forward with them during the invitation. Urge them to make a public testimony of their faith in Christ and to be baptized.

19. Stay in contact. Involve them in ministry. Continue to maintain a relationship and encourage them. Invite them to be trained as soul-winners. They too need to go and lead others to Jesus.

Factor #32
Churches and people never grow until they go.

Ask yourself:

- Am I willing to share the gospel?
- Will I maintain a relationship with those who accept Christ?
- What is my church doing to equip people to go?

Pray...

— for a desire to go and visit the lost.

— for someone to go with you.

— for the lost that will be saved as a result of your visits.

— for your church to grow by going.

THE MASTER'S COMMISSION

Larry Kerychuk saw that many young people had no direction in their lives until the age of twenty-five. So I released him to create the Master's Commission, where young people who desire to serve God enter into a training program. For one year these young people dedicate their lives to Bible study and hands-on ministry.

They pray, memorize scripture, learn doctrine and study about ministry. They also put into practice what they are learning by visiting nursing homes to conduct services, ministering to the needy, witnessing to the lost and helping in our many ministries. They become an army of disciples. It's like having 120 ministers on staff.

The Master's Commission has multiplied disciples, and hundreds of young people have been equipped for ministry.

Graduates of the Master's Commission have become youth pastors, evangelists, and pastors all over America and throughout the world. Four pastors on staff in Phoenix came from our Master's Commission.

Now, all the Master's Commissions around the country network with one another to continue to share ideas and improve the ministry of equipping.

Factor #33

Use a New Kind of Deacon to Involve People in Ministry

> But unto every one of us is given grace according to the measure of the gift of Christ (Eph. 4:7).

If people are not involved in ministry, some debilitating symptoms arise in a church:

- Uninvolved people use their time criticizing others instead of edifying others.
- Uninvolved people miss God moving and doing miracles in their midst.
- Uninvolved people lose the joy of leading the lost to Christ.
- Uninvolved people become frustrated, angry and eventually inactive.

How do we involve people in ministry? In our congregation, we train and equip a new kind of deacon to care for the church.

During our parade of ministry at a Pastors' School, 6,000 people walked across our platform with signs describing scores of our ministsries. Viewing this parade of ministries, an insight came to Dr. Hurston. He had started Dr. Cho's cell ministry in Seoul, Korea. After the service, Dr. Hurston commented to me, "The reason Dr. Cho has such a great church is not only because of the wonderful cell ministries but because of 50,000 deaconnesses and deacons. Those 6,000 people I saw walking across your platform are really your deacons and deaconnesses."

So I went to my deacon board and asked them to become an administrative board and to let me establish visitation deacons and deaconnesses. Each of them has fifteen families to visit twice a year.

Here are the important factors they use in visitation to involve others in ministry.

1. **Make contact with people.** Every deacon leader regularly contacts fifteen family units — individuals or couples, including any children. We love them, pray for their needs, nurture them and work hard to involve them in a ministry. Involved people are happy people in the church.

2. **Talent and gift evaluations.** We find out where the interests and gifts of other people lie. Talents must be used, or fulfillment and challenge is lost in a church.

3. **Overcome any excuses others may have for not being involved.** As deacons work with the group they are nurturing, they form accountability relationships. They learn about the real lives of those under their care. And they get to know each person under their care so that they will be able to counteract any excuse another person may have for not being involved in a ministry that fits him.

4. **Inform people of the *"four W's."*** Deacons know the *who, what, when* and *where* of every meeting, event, service and ministry of the church. Now that is a big order in a church with over two hundred ministries. If a deacon cannot answer a specific question or need that arises within their group, they know where to go and whom to ask to

get the information.

5. Never make promises you cannot keep. There are many helping ministries in our church. We can point people to the right ministry, but we cannot specifically promise what that ministry will be able to do for each individual. Each person needs to follow the biblical process of asking, seeking and knocking in order to find answers and ministry fulfillment.

6. Display a helpful — not helpless — attitude. A deacon's vocabulary should not include the phrase, "Well, I don't know." A leader may not have the information at his fingertips, but he is always ready and willing to find out the needed information as soon as possible.

7. When in doubt, refer. At various times all of us encounter needs and questions that go beyond our ability to minister to or answer. A person may have a physical or spiritual need that a deacon simply cannot meet. A person may have an emotional need that requires counseling or guidance. A person may have a concern or doctrinal question that only a pastor can answer. When a leader is beyond his or her own abilities, gifts and skills, that leader acts wisely and refers the needy person to someone who can minister to the need.

8. Always be soul-conscious. A deacon or church leader must always be sensitive to what is happening with people spiritually. A person's eternal relationship with Jesus Christ as Lord and Savior is the primary concern. A leader is always ready to give an account of the hope within him (1 Peter 3:15); he or she is always ready to share the gospel or pray with another person.

MULTIPLICATION

Factor #33
Leaders involve people in ministry.

Ask yourself:

- Am I a candidate to be a deacon or leader in the church?
- Who is nurturing me? To whom am I accountable in our church?
- As a leader, am I nurturing and involving others in ministry?

Pray...

— to become the leader God desires you to be.

— for those that you nurture and care for in the church.

Factor #34

Personalize Ministry

> Take heed to the ministry which thou hast received in the Lord, that thou fulfill it (Col. 4:17).

Personalization is vital for effective ministry. Personalization is simply leaders forming personal relationships with people in a congregation so that they can be effectively ministered to and nurtured. We cannot help or disciple another Christian unless we have a personal relationship with that individual. Personalization also mean individualization. Each person is special and unique. No two relationships are identically alike. The way a leader nurtures one person may not work with another. We must be sensitive to the needs and concerns of each person.

After winning people to Christ, win people to yourself.

Be careful not to misunderstand what I am saying. I am not saying that you seek to win people to yourself for the purpose of manipulation, control or dependency. I am saying that, like Paul, "To the weak became I as weak, that I might gain the weak. I am made all things to all men, that I might by all means save some" (1 Cor. 9:22). Paul encouraged others to follow the example set by himself and Christian leaders (2 Thess. 3:9). You can encourage others to follow your example as you follow Christ.

As leaders develop personal, caring relationships with people in the church, they will find themselves relating to three categories of individuals.

1. Inactive People

These people are the hardest to involve in ministry and to develop a relationship with. Often their motivation for coming to church is to be entertained. They are spectators in a non-spectator arena. They come to watch worship instead of worshiping. They want the gifts and not the Giver. They follow after signs and wonders instead of having signs and wonders follow after them. They want the message to do something for them instead of going out and living the message. These are the hardest people to nurture because they are constantly taking and never giving. When a leader finds himself or herself spending too much time trying to develop in-depth relationships with these people, that leader will become frustrated and burn out.

Inactive people have become lukewarm in their relationship with Christ. They have forgotten their first love. Help them to fall in love again with fresh fire and passion for Jesus Christ.

2. Active People

These individuals are church members who receive nurturing and guidance. They desire personal contact with leadership. Be wise in your guidance of active people. Involve them in ministry that fits their talents and gifts.

Urge them to do a few ministries well and with excellence instead of trying to be everywhere, go to everything and do everything.

Initially guide active people to one ministry such as a class or home group that helps them to grow spiritually. Help them find a ministry that encourages spiritual growth through an outreach such as visiting a prison, hospital or home. They may be able to minister through a teaching or music ministry. Active Christians need at least one ministry that feeds them and one ministry that equips and uses them to minister to others. I am not saying that you should limit a person to one giving and one receiving ministry. Individuals can become involved in more ministries as time permits and training equips.

3. Unsaved people

Yes, in every group that a leader nurtures in a church there may be unsaved people. Do not assume that just because people attend church and use religious language they are saved. Always be ready to lead a person to Jesus Christ.

The Importance of Watchmen and Teams

Church leaders are to be *watchmen* for Christ. They notice people. Jesus had a wonderful ministry of noticing people. He did not walk around in a divine daze. He noticed the paralyzed man as he lay beside the pool. He noticed the blind man on the side of the road. He noticed a crowd growing hungry as they listened to Him teach.

When leaders are caring for and nurturing church members, they notice when a person misses worship or experiences sickness, success and various life passages such as birthdays, anniversaries or graduations. Leadership acts upon what they notice with affirmation, prayer, cards, phone calls, visits and personal contact.

Finally, leaders who personalize their nurturing of church members understand that they themselves are part of a *team.* Leaders are not lone rangers who work alone. They are accountable to one another through prayer and discipleship. Leaders nurture and support one another. Jesus sent out leaders two by two. He formed a team of twelve men to work with Him. He understood that if we are left to ourselves, at times we will become discouraged and fail to function properly. Pastors, leaders, elders, deacons and all church leaders need to be a part of leadership teams that nurture, pray for, and equip one another and hold each other accountable in Christ.

Factor #34
Leaders personalize ministry by caring for people.

Ask yourself:

- Am I part of a team that trains, nurtures and holds me accountable?
- Who are the people I am nurturing, and in which category are they — inactive, active or unsaved?
- How can I personalize my relationship with each person I am nurturing and discipling in the church?

Factor #34

Pray...

— for those you are leading, nurturing and discipling.

— to be a Christ-like example that others can follow.

— for those on the leadership team with you.

Love and a Drive-By Shooting

A young black boy was shot and killed by a gang on the steps of the Dream Center. Matthew took up an offering that night during the youth meeting. After the youth meeting, he took the $29 offering and walked across the street to the home of the slain child's mother.

Gang members filled the place with tension as Matthew softly spoke to the grieving mother. "We took up an offering for you. We want to give it to you to let you know that we love you."

As he left, the gang member guarding the door asked, "Could you pray with me?"

As Matthew prayed, the gang leader repeated Matthew's prayer in Spanish. Gang members joined hands as he prayed for everyone in the room to accept Jesus Christ.

From that night Matthew and other church members have been safe in that neighborhood. Their cars and property are protected. The gang members have begun coming to church and bringing their gang brothers with them. Soon many were saved and discipled.

The entire neighborhood was transformed by the love of Christ.

That first act of love has multiplied into the salvation of people throughout the surrounding neighborhood.

Factor #35

The Overflow of Leadership

> And there was also a strife among them, which of them should be accounted the greatest. And he said unto them, The kings of the Gentiles exercise lordship over them; and they that exercise authority upon them are called benefactors. But ye shall not be so: but he that is greatest among you, let him be as the younger; and he that is chief, as he that doth serve. For whether is greater, he that sitteth at meat, or he that serveth? Is not he that sitteth at meat? But I [Jesus] am among you as he that serveth (Luke 22:24-27).

Leaders have *strength* that others do not have. A leader is one who has an excess of what others lack. So others are able to draw from leaders without draining them. Others grow stronger when they follow a leader. Jesus had strength that no other human being ever had. He used His strength to serve others and make them strong.

Leaders also have *truth* that others do not have. They possess a knowledge of the truth that others desire to hear, understand and obey. Jesus not only had the truth, He was truth (John 14:6). His life so applied and embodied truth that those who follow Him also live and walk in truth.

Leaders have a *holiness* that others do not have. Others

gain holiness from the overflow of holiness in leaders' lives. When other people are in the presence of a holy leader, they feel the presence of God. Jesus had perfect holiness. When in His presence, His followers are also in the Father's presence (John 10:30).

When we as leaders become servants like Christ, we put on Christ (Rom. 13:14). As we follow Him, we put on His strength, truth and holiness. As we serve others in Jesus' name (Matt. 25:31-46), we overflow with the life of Christ through His Spirit into the lives of others.

Leaders must ask, "Do we overflow with God's Spirit into the lives of others?"

A leader overflowing with the Spirit is anointed by God to lead. The anointing of the Holy Spirit refers to the imparting of God's power upon a person to minister and lead others. The anointing does not accompany a position but rather a calling. If a person occupies a position in the church without the anointing of God's Spirit, there will be no power to lead. Only when a person walks in God's calling, serving as Christ serves, does the anointing rest upon him or her as a leader.

Throughout the ages, great spiritual leaders have had times when they experienced the power of God coming upon them to lead. In the Bible, priests, prophets and kings were anointed to lead and serve God's people. Jesus was the Christ, the Messiah, the "Anointed One." As our Priest, Prophet and King, Jesus anoints Christians to lead by His power and authority. Without His anointing, there is no power to lead. Without His calling, there is no anointing. Without becoming a servant like the suffering Servant, we have no calling. Without taking up the cross and following Him, we will never become servants.

True leadership begins by serving as Christ served and results in a powerful anointing to minister as Christ ministered (John 14:12).

Leaders experience the power of His anointing to lead others when they serve others as Christ served.

Factor #35

True leaders that lead are truly servants that serve.

Ask yourself:

- Am I a servant like Jesus Christ?
- Am I serving and walking in my calling?
- Is my motive to lead rooted not in a desire for position but rather in a desire to serve?

Pray...

— to become a servant.

— and humble yourself before God and others.

— for His anointing to become a servant leader.

Factor #36

Let Preachers Preach

> For after that in the wisdom of God the world by wisdom knew not God, it pleased God by the foolishness of preaching to save them that believe (1 Cor. 1:21).

Churches that multiply disciples have preachers who do not listen to man but to God. Preachers are called to live by the high standards of righteousness and holiness. God used preachers to scatter the gospel abroad everywhere (Acts 8:4).

The foolishness of preaching has been ordained by God to spread the gospel. The demise of denominations and churches is directly related to the demise of preaching. Preaching is teaching with tears in your eyes. Preaching is truth on fire. Preaching is the Word of God in your hand. Preaching is the fire of God in your heart. Preaching is the gift of God wrapped in a voice filled with excitement and zeal. Preaching is the moral conscience of a city and a nation. There's a holy power behind preaching that the Holy Spirit uses to touch the hearts of people and bring conviction, repentance and revival.

If a church is to multiply disciples, the preacher must be constrained by the love of Christ to preach the gospel above all else (2 Cor. 5:14). To be *constrained* means there is a narrowing effect on ministry if you are a preacher. Paul emphasized that one thing became a priority in his life, one thing possessed him. What was it? He was consumed with a passion to preach the gospel so that the Jews *and* gentiles might be saved.

Paul was pressed on every side to do many things but the passion of proclaiming the gospel consumed him. There is a lesson in Paul's example for preachers whose churches are multiplying. The preacher cannot do everything in the church. He cannot do everything he is asked to do or expected to do in the church or the community.

When I began pastoring in Davenport, I did the preaching, the teaching, the pastoring, the counseling, the hospital visitation and the office typing. I had to do it all. I had to lead the choir and work with the youth. But as the work grew, I found that my prayer time and study of the Word was suffering. I had to be constrained. Others had to be trained and equipped to teach, work with the youth, lead the choir and visit. Yes, all those ministries were important, but there was a priority for me on preaching.

I learned that people can love more than one leader in a congregation. As the responsibility of growing a church gets bigger, the people have to grow. More pastors may be needed, and lay leaders will need to be released. People will love and encourage them just as they do the preacher. God's man needs time to go to the mountain and pray; time to study and meditate on God's Word; time to soak in the presence of God; time for family and rest. The pastor also must grow with the church. The church cannot become big without a *big* pastor. He must always grow.

It's time for preachers to decide what constrains them and to narrow down their ministries to proclaim the gospel through "the foolishness of preaching" (see 1 Cor. 1:21).

Factor #36

Churches that grow release the preacher to preach the gospel without human restraint.

Ask yourself:

- What priority has our congregation placed upon the preaching of the Word?
- Does the preacher in our congregation have the support he or she needs to spend time with God and to do all that is required to preach the gospel?

Pray...

— that the preacher in your congregation is so constrained by the love of Christ that preaching the gospel become a top priority for his or her time.

— that your church will allow the preacher the liberty to preach the gospel without human restraint.

FROM A BUSLOAD TO THOUSANDS IN SIDEWALK SUNDAY SCHOOLS

As a young man, Bill Wilson caught a vision for bus ministry after he heard me speak in 1978. From one leftover bus from a recent Vacation Bible School, he launched a bus ministry in St. Petersburg, Florida.

Abandoned by his mother at a curb, Bill longed to reach the forgotten children of the inner cities of America.

He became the director of my bus ministry in Davenport, Iowa. One day he came to me and said, "I know you have always wanted to go to New York City. Now I am going to go there and represent you." His ministry at Metro Church has mutliplied to reach more than 15,000 kids weekly through his Sidewalk Sunday School bus ministry.

Bill has networked with us at the Dream Center in Los Angeles, where his ministry reaches thousands of children weekly.

His ministry has multiplied around the world in far-flung places such as the Philippines and South Africa. From one broken-down bus in St. Petersburg, God has used the ministry of Bill Wilson to multiply disciples throughout the world — especially in children's ministry.

FACTOR #37

Live From the Inside Out

> He that believeth on me, as the scripture hath said, out of his heart shall flow rives of living water. [But this spake (Jesus) of the Spirit, which they that believe on him should receive: for the Holy Ghost was not yet given; because that Jesus was not yet glorified.] (John 7:38-39).

There is a whole new world for churches and Christians who will live from the inside out. There is no problem too big, no attack too destructive and no obstacle too massive when the flow in our lives comes from the indwelling Holy Spirit.

When the Holy Spirit directs all that the church and God's people do from the inside out, then what happens outside the house doesn't matter. The house is built on solid ground. When we flow from the inside out, we are strong and secure in God's leading.

The bigger my problem and the greater my battle, then the earlier I rise to pray in the morning. The Spirit within me takes control, and He that is in me is greater than anything outside of me (1 John 4:4).

You may protest saying that I am approaching life's difficulties too simplistically. The truth is, life is simple! The outward flow of the Spirit in prayer creates the strength and power to overcome the world (see Rom. 8).

Living within you is the omnipotent, omniscient and

omnipresent God. Dwelling within you is the Holy Spirit, who by His very nature is God. So you can live from the inside out. As He flows from the inside out, healing flows into the soul, mind, heart and body.

Churches that multiply disciples live from the inside out. When they let the outside in, the infections of strife, conflict and dissension begin to fester.

Let's suppose you forget who you are in Christ and begin living from the outside in. When that happens you or your church will be reactive instead of proactive. You will be defensive instead of offensive for Jesus Christ. You will become a victim instead of a victor.

Living from the inside out depends on prayer and the Word of God. Without the Word and prayer, the rivers flowing from within will dry up. So will our strength, power and growth.

Whenever we allow something on the outside to become our source, the true, inner source of the Spirit will dissipate. I have heard people comment, "I tried to worship in that church but there was no life there." What they are saying is that the inner flow from the Holy Spirit is stopped up. Old wells with polluted water cannot refresh people and empower the church.

What stops the river, the wellspring of the Holy Spirit, from flowing through us and our churches? Sometimes our wells get clogged. Here are four things that can stop them up.

1. Unmet needs.

When church members have unmet needs, the inner flow begins to trickle and finally to stop. Churches that fail to meet the authentic needs of people for God's Word, for His presence in praise and worship or for His power in work and service find themselves turning to the world for methods and gimmicks instead of to Christ who meets every need.

2. Unfulfilled expectations.

When churches proclaim God's dreams and vision for their congregation and then depart from His ways, the people react in worldly ways, missing God's Spirit who fulfills every God-given expectation.

3. Unhealed hurts.

Too often church people hurt each other and then fail to forgive and be reconciled to one another. Forgiveness flows from the Spirit within and becomes the healing balm for church hurts. Without the Spirit's flow of forgiving mercy and grace, unhealed hurts will divide and split churches.

4. Unconfessed sins.

James 5 instructs us to confess our sins to one another. Repentance and confession keeps the church healed and healthy. Without confession and repentance prompted by the convicting Spirit within, a church will depart from holiness and righteousness while compromising truth and tolerating sin.

When a church lets people, money, power or methods become its source instead of the indwelling Spirit, life ebbs from the congregation and multiplying growth stops.

Factor #37
Churches living from the inside out overflow with the Spirit's life into the lives of others.

Ask yourself:

- Am I reacting to the world or living from the inside out?
- Is my church flowing with life from the wellspring of God's Spirit?

Pray...

— for the power of the indwelling Spirit to flow into your life.

— for life to flow out of your church into the lives of God's people and those in the world.

Factor #38

Begin by Loving Souls

> For God so loved the world that he gave his only begotten Son, that whosoever believeth in him should not perish, but have everlasting life (John 3:16).

Before we teach people how to *win* souls, we need to teach them how to *love* souls. Before we can learn how to win the lost, we must love them as God loves them.

There is no true love for the lost except the love that comes from the Holy Spirit. We do not learn to love the lost. No course or motivating sermon can fill us with true tears for the lost. Only the living Spirit of God can fill us with both love and tears for the lost.

What brings a church to the crossroads of both loving and weeping for the lost? Only when love and tears mix are God's people ready to be equipped for winning the lost to Christ. Here are some practical ways to allow God's Spirit to give your church tears and love for the lost:

1. Preach about God's love for the lost.

If we fail to emphasize the Great Commission and God's love for the lost from our pulpits, we miss the opportunity to place the highest priority in the church on soul-winning.

2. Recall how much God loved us when we were lost.

Past memories often become the power that gives rise to poignant memories which evoke genuine tears of thanksgiving.

3. Have big events that invite the lost to the church.

Such events will allow church members the opportunity to both invite and minister to the unsaved.

4. Pray for the lost.

Prayer meetings, small groups and special times of prayer and fasting for the lost open God's people up to the Holy Spirit, giving them the opportunity to be filled with love and tears for the lost.

There are precious times for weeping in the life of a church that desires to multiply disciples. One of those times is at the altar of repentance when the unsaved come to accept Christ and the saved come to confess their lack of love for the lost.

Another time of weeping happens when the Holy Spirit reveals the hopelessness, despair, loneliness, pain and hurt of the lost. Then we can weep with Christ for those who are outside of His kingdom. and we can know His heart of love for the unsaved.

Only a love for the lost will prepare us to be equipped in soul-winning. And only tears for the lost will wash away our fears, busyness and apathy. Perhaps our churches today need to spend more time in praying, weeping and loving the lost before they rush into soul-winning seminars and classes.

Factor #38
Soul-winning begins by loving souls.

Ask yourself:

- Do I love the lost?
- Is my church weeping for and loving the unsaved?

Pray...

— that the Holy Spirit will grow a deep love within you for the lost.

— that your church will grow in its love and weeping for the lost.

Church On The Street

Upon arriving at Phoenix First Assembly, Walt Latray came to me saying, "Do you care if I take the buses that you use on Sunday morning to pick up people and bring them to church on Sunday night?" he asked me.

I replied, "Go ahead."

The first night he brought a busload, one drunk man sauntered to the pulpit and started preaching before the service. Later Walt said to me, "Well, I suppose you don't want us back next week."

"Come back next week, and bring ten times as many people from the streets," I replied. So in the next weeks he brought more and more. He filled up every one of the small missions in town with people who were being saved from the streets.

I said to Walt, "Let's get you your own place for ministry." So we bought him the first house for the Church on the Street ministry. He now has fourteen houses, two church buildings and is about to buy a warehouse that will house more people.

This man reaches 3,500 people weekly in his downtown ministry.

He reaches people out of the prisons and off the streets, putting people in the homes, restoring them and finding them jobs.

There are now Church on the Street ministries all over America.

Factor #39

Givers Multiply — Takers Divide

> I have showed you all things, how that so laboring ye ought to support the weak, and to remember the words of the Lord Jesus, how he said, It is more blessed to give than to receive (Acts 20:35).

The early church in Acts multiplied disciples with astounding success. By the way, it was filled with givers. That is no coincidence. Givers multiply while hoarders divide and decrease numbers. A church filled with givers will multiply disciples. Consider the evidence of the early church.

- They had all things in common.

  > And all that believed were together, and had all things common; and sold their possessions and goods, and parted them to all men, as every man had need (Acts 2:44-45).

- There was no lack as a result of their giving.

  > Neither was there any among them that lacked: for as many as were possessors of lands or houses sold them, and brought the prices of the things that were sold, and laid them down at the apostles' feet: and distribution was made unto every man according as he had need (Acts 4:34-35).

As the church gave, it multiplied. But when the law of self-preservation invaded the church, problems immediately arose. Ananias and Sapphira had promised God that if they sold their property they would give it all to God. They had consecrated their gift to the Lord. Be careful about what you vow.

Many people run around making this commitment and that. They vow to God to consecrate a certain gift or talent or time to the Lord. Then they try to touch that which is sacred to God. The law of self-preservation sets in and they try to possess that which belongs to God.

Ananias and Sapphira made a promise to God to give (see Acts 5). But they held back on their promise, giving only part of their gift while pretending to give it all. Such deceit is lying to the Holy Spirit. As a result of their allowing the law of self-preservation to take priority over God in their lives, they died. Jesus said, "For whosoever will save his life shall lose it: and whosoever will lose his life for my sake shall find it. For what is a man profited, if he shall gain the whole world, and lose his own soul? Or what shall a man give in exchange for his soul?" (Matt. 16:25-26).

Churches, like people, have only two lifestyles to embrace — giving or taking. Churches filled with givers are giving churches. Such churches give to their people and to their cities with such joy that both giver and recipients are blessed. The unsaved take notice of those who give without thought of self-preservation.

However, some churches put up walls and protect what little they have accumulated. Like bank vaults, they take and hoard but rarely give and bless.

As long as people and churches give they will be filled, and the miracle of multiplication will continue. As soon as there are no more gifts to give or vessels to fill, the multiplication ceases.

When the early Christians gave all that they had to God, no one lacked anything in their midst. But when one couple decided to hoard what they had, life ceased. Instead of multiplication, great fear came upon all the church (Acts 5:11).

Each year our congregation gives away thousands of turkeys at Thanksgiving. I ask each member to bring a frozen turkey. This year we gave four thousand turkeys away. What a blessing we receive from giving to others! Giving is a way of life in our congregation. We give to the poor in our city and to those in Los Angeles and around the world. We give to thousands of pastors around the nation through our Pastors' Conference each year. We give through the Master's Commission to train and equip leaders for the church. We give through more than two hundred ministry outreaches. We have discovered that as we empty ourselves in giving, God pours into our lives even more abundantly. We are now reaping in due season from our giving.

The law of self-preservation leads to death in people and in churches. Ananias and Sapphira died instantly when they withheld the promised gift. A miracle is really a healing that is speeded up — the time span has been compressed, and healing happens quickly. With Ananias and Sapphira, the death process was speeded up. When they ceased to become givers, they experienced suddenly what all takers and hoarders eventually experience — death. The church that gives, multiplies.

Factor #39
Only givers multiply.

Ask yourself:

- Am I a taker or a giver?
- Is my church experiencing abundance or lack?
- How can I grow joyfully and cheerfully in my giving?

Pray...

— to become a giver, not a taker.

— for your church to become a giving church.

Factor #40

Not Safe — But It's Good

> And the news about them reached the ears of the church at Jerusalem, and they sent Barnabas off to Antioch. Then when he had come and witnessed the grace of God, he rejoiced and began to encourage them all with resolute heart to remain true to the Lord; for he was a good man and full of the Holy Spirit and faith. And considerable numbers were brought to the Lord. And he left for Tarsus to look for Saul; and when he had found him, he brought him to Antioch. And it came about that for an entire year they met with the church, and taught considerable numbers; and the disciples were first called Christians in Antioch (Acts 11:22-26, NAS).

In C. S. Lewis' *Chronicles of Narnia,* one of the little girls, Lucy, is describing to a friend what the lion, Asland, is like. After she described this mighty lion who represents Christ in the allegory, her friend said, "Oh, I trust that I never want to see him."

Lucy replied, "You do not understand. If you ever saw him, you would want to run to him. And you would want to put your arms around his neck and bury your face in his mane and never want to leave him."

Lucy's friend mused, "Oh, you mean he's safe?"

And Lucy, with a horror in her eyes, responded, "No, he's not safe — but he's good!"

Observe closely this community of Christians at Antioch and you will recognize Lucy's philosophy in their lives. They were a rich, strong, Spirit-filled, blood-washed congregation of believers. God had given them a core of leaders, or staff members if you please, of such richness and depth that their names are recorded in the holy Scripture for our benefit two thousand years later. Imagine that!

One morning as this staff prayed together, the Holy Spirit spoke to them, "Take Barnabas and Saul and carve them away from your ministry. Carve them away from this church of Antioch for I have a special missionary purpose for them to accomplish."

Imagine how threatening this is! The Holy Spirit changed and challenged the status quo. His request was going to weaken the staff and the church. Saul and Barnabas were the best two staff members. Saul was an intelligent genius. Barnabas, whose very name means "son of encouragement, was the most loving and tender of them all."

God has the right and the power and the authority to break into our personal lives, families, homes, churches or ministries at any moment, declaring that He has a fresh direction for His church. God's ideas are always good but rarely safe. Now that's threatening.

The Holy Spirit has declared Himself as the authority of change in our lives and our churches. No matter how close you are to God, God wants you closer. No matter how rich your prayer life is, God wants it richer. No matter how far into sin, how hard, rebellious and disobedient you are, God wants you saved. And if you are saved, He wants you sanctified. And if you are sanctified, He wants you filled with the Holy Spirit. And if you are filled with the Holy Spirit, He wants you to be exhibiting the fruits of the Spirit. And if the fruits of the Spirit are manifested in your life, He wants to use you in ministry. There is one song that every Christian ought to sing:

Lord, lift me up and let me stand
By faith on heaven's tableland.
A higher plane than I have found —
Lord, plant my feet on higher ground.

God's higher ground is not safe but it's good.

Churches that multiply are not "playing it safe." None of the factors that you have read in this book are guaranteed to be safe. Multiplication involves risk. On many Thursday evenings in Los Angeles, I board one of our buses to make the weekly ride to Skid Row. On each bus, a team of four or five people from our church hits the streets to invite bums, prostitutes, drug addicts, the homeless, derelicts and assorted types of criminals to church. One street that I walk regularly on these visitations has the highest murder rate of any single street in the city. What we are doing is not safe, but it's good.

Each week I have the privilege of seeing scores of these "unsafe" people from the streets come to the altar at LAIC and be saved, delivered, healed and set free.

The entire ministry venture in Los Angeles is not safe, but it's good. As this book draws to its conclusion, we still must pay over $1 million dollars for the property in L.A. and we have less than a month to raise those funds. For over a year we have invested people, time and money into over one hundred ministries in Los Angeles before we completely owned the property. We had permission to occupy and begin renovations and ministry before completing the final payment.

In some ways that is how we all do ministry. We may think we own our buildings, programs and ministries but we do not. Nothing ever done in genuine ministry is completely safe. All that we have and do belongs to God. Yes, we have taken enormous risks to build a ministry in Los Angeles. The land and facilities do not belong to us. But when we make that final payment, they still will not be ours — everything belongs to the Lord. We are called to be stewards not owners. We have permission to occupy but not to possess. Such an approach to ministry is not safe, but it's good.

Our congregation in Phoenix allows me to travel across this country weekly, preaching and sharing about the Dream Center with churches everywhere. That was risky for our church. But we have experienced the greatest spiritual revival, greatest harvest of souls and greatest financial blessings ever in our church during this time of greatest risk. Not one person came to me and criticized the "unsafe" approach we were taking.

So how do I control the risks? My reply is, "I don't. If He can build His church, then He can keep it." I always want to be a part of a church that can sense the presence of the Holy Spirit in our midst. There is no set formula for multiplication. But there is an atmosphere for it. That atmosphere is charged with the presence of the Holy Spirit and filled with a people yearning to be used by Him. The climate of a multiplying church continually changes, confronting people with unsafe and risky weather. No record exists of anyone ever walking on water without a storm, some wind and a lot of risk. The territory between the boat and Jesus is miracle territory. And the only way to traverse miracle territory is by trusting the Savior not the ship.

We do not get miracles because we *want* them. We get miracles because we *need* them.

It's at that moment when you must walk on water through a storm, and you know it's impossible, that you cry out, "Lord, help me!" You desperately need a miracle.

And God says, "Good. I've been waiting for you to say that. I'm going to bring situations now in which you will be so desperate for a miracle that you will trust me."

What God is saying to you and me is, "If you'll step out of the boat, walk out on the watera and take a leap of faith, I'll release supernatural power in just the right measure at the right moment." *It's not safe, but it's good.*

Factor #40
Churches that multiply are not safe — but they are good!!

Ask yourself:

- Am I more concerned with being safe than with experiencing the full goodness of God?
- Is my church taking risks with God to reach the world for Jesus Christ?

Pray...

— that God will give you the courage to take risks for His sake.

— that your church will follow Christ no matter how "unsafe" the journey might be.

Life Conquers Death

Danny Shoemaker, a minister at the Dream Center, has terminal cancer from an inoperative brain tumor. He had started eight churches in Africa and wanted to go back. When he couldn't return, Danny became involved in the Dream Center. Danny and the Dream Center flowed together with a common destiny. The experts had pronounced a death sentence on both the inner city of Los Angeles and upon Danny. However, God defies the experts. He brings life out of death.

Today Danny Shoemaker ministers life to the lost and dying on the streets of Los Angeles. He rides the buses to Skid Row and traverses the mammoth Dream Center campus spreading hugs, encouragement and love to old-timers and newcomers alike.

He's actually giving his life in the inner city of Los Angeles.

No one but the Lord knows how many more weeks Danny will live on this earth. But Danny knows that he will live eternally. He is multiplying his faith in Christ into scores of other people. Out of death, Danny brings eternal life, hope and love to a city once thought dead. Danny will finish strong!

Postscript

Finish Strong!

Most people who read this book have heard of Billy Graham, but what about Chuck Templeton? What about Bron Clifford? Have you ever heard of them? Did you know that they were also packing out auditoriums in 1945 when Billy Graham first preached to large crowds? I want to share with you some thoughts prompted by the book *Finishing Strong* by Steve Farrar.

All three of these young men rose to prominence in their middle twenties. One seminary president, after hearing Chuck Templeton — a brilliant, dynamic preacher — called him the most gifted, talented young preacher in America. Templeton and Graham became very close friends. They started preaching together with the Youth for Christ organization. Most observers thought that Templeton would be the one who would go to the top. One magazine wrote a feature article calling Templeton the "Babe Ruth of evangelism."

Bron Clifford was another gifted, young fireball evangelist. Many believed that Clifford was the most gifted, powerful preacher to come up in the church for many centuries. People lined up for hours to hear him preach. When he went to Baylor University to give a discourse, they actually cut the ropes of the bells of the tower. They wanted nothing to interfere with his preaching. For two and a half hours the students of Baylor sat on the edges of their seats as he gave a dissertation on "Christ and the Philosopher's Stone." At age twenty-five, Clifford touched more lives, influenced more leaders and set more attendance records than any other clergyman in American history. National leaders vied for his attention. He was tall, handsome, dashing, intelligent, sophisticated and intelligent. Hollywood actually tried to cast him in the lead role for the famous movie, *The Robe.* He seemed to have everything.

Graham, Templeton and Clifford launched out of the starting block like Olympic gold medalists in 1945. Why haven't you heard of Chuck Templeton or Bron Clifford? The answer may surprise you.

By 1950 Templeton had left the ministry. He pursued a radio career. He became an announcer and a newscaster, telling the world that he no longer believed Jesus Christ was the Son of God. He became an atheist. By 1950, this future Babe Ruth of preaching was not even in the ball game.

By 1954 Clifford had lost his family, ministry and health. Eventually he lost his life because of addiction to alcohol. Financial irresponsibility left his wife and their two Downs-syndrome children penniless. This once famous preacher died of cirrhosis of the liver at the age of thirty-five in a rundown hotel on the edge of Amarillo, Texas. He died unwept, unhonored and unsung. Some pastors from Amarillo, Texas, got together and collected enough money to buy a cheap casket. They shipped his body back to the East Coast, where he was buried in a pauper's cemetery.

In 1945 all three of these young men with extraordinary gifts were preaching for the purpose of multiplying the church by thousands of people. But within ten years only one of them was still on track for Christ.

In the Christian life it's not how you start; it's how you finish. A recent survey shocked me, it reported that only one out of ten who start in ministry at the age of twenty-one serve the Lord to age sixty-five. They fall away from ministry due to immorality, discouragement, liberal theology and a love for wealth and the things of this world.

You may be saying "Pastor Barnett, this is really an interesting story — the statistics are intriguing — but I cannot relate to it because I'm not in the ministry." May I rock your boat by suggesting that if you are a Christian and are serious about Jesus Christ, then you are in the ministry. All Christians are in ministry (see Eph. 4:11; Col. 3:23). Whatever your profession, you work for Jesus. Jesus said that you are the salt of the earth and the light of the world (Matt. 5:13-14). You are the only thing flavoring and saving this world. We are coworkers with Christ.

Here are my questions to you:

- Will you finish strong for Christ?
- Will you be a multiplier for Him throughout your life?
- What will keep you from being one who leaves the race?

You see, those who finish strong are the exceptions. Why? Because when it comes to finishing strong, there are so many odds against you. The devil is against you and so are the flesh and the cares of this world. You could become your own worst enemy as you place your personal wants and desires above seeking the kingdom of God. Although not impossible, finishing strong is improbable. You will be required to make some tough choices.

The church needs Christians committed to the call of Christ and the Great Commission. Such Christians will choose...

- marriage and family over divorce and brokenness;
- teaching children God's ways not the world's ways;
- people over policies and programs;
- enlarging instead of reducing their circles of love;
- risking much for God rather than playing it safe.

To finish strong, we must choose...

- to multiply not just add disciples,
- to stand for truth when critics are the loudest;
- to release not control people in ministry;
- and to pray and fast and pray again.

Multiplication is the last great end-time revival. Reaping will come quicker than we can sow. Harvest time will require more work and workers than we can imagine. And the risks will be greater than anyone has ever undertaken. God continues to ask the soul-winning, soul-searching question, "Whom shall I send?"

Those who finish strong are needed more than ever as the church multiplies disciples in the last days. Multitudes await the gospel. Will you be the multiplier proclaiming the good news of Jesus Christ who goes to the waiting masses? I urge you to respond to God's call, "Here am I; send me." Go and finish strong for Christ!

Appendix 1:
Phoenix First Assembly — Ministries List

A Child's Heart Puppet Ministry
Adoption for Christmas
Adult Choir
Adult Christian Education
Aerobics
AIDS Ministry
Alvin R. Booher Library
Americans for Decency
Assembly Homeschoolers
Athletes International Ministries
Audio
Audit Committee
Banquets
Baptismal Service (WM's)
Bereavement Ministry (Heaven's Connection)
Board of Directors
Bookstore
Boys & Girls Missionary Crusade
Bread Basket Ministry
Brunch/Speakers Fellowship
Building Maintenance
Bulletin Board
Bus Mechanics
Bus Ministry
Castle of the King
Celebration Productions
Centurion Careers
Child Care
Children's Choir
Children's Church (1st to 6th grade)
Christian Education (1st to 6th grade)
Christian Men's Network
Church In the Son
Church On the Street
Church Architecture Ministry
Church On the Street Men's Homes
City Conquest
Coffee House
College & Career Prayer
College & Career Fellowship Families
College & Career Cross Examination
Community Service Ministry
Construction Volunteers
Conventions & Visitors
COPS Ministry
Corporate Prayer Ministry
Costuming Ministry
Creative Media Productions
Crime Victims Ministry
Crisis Hot-Line
Cross Country Worship Team
Custodians
Day Care Visitation Teams
Deacon Ministry
Deaf Culture Ministry
Door Greeters
Drama For Productions
Early Childhood Ministry (Infant — Kindergarten)
Exaltation!
Excel
Executive Paging & Information
Fashion Share
Financial Planning

MULTIPLICATION

Fine Arts Festival
Fitness Center
Food Commissary (WM's)
Forsaken Not
Funeral (WM's)
Golf Cart Ministry (Mobile Greeters)
Gospel Car-Go
Graphic Art
Grooming Ministry
Grounds Keepers
Gymnasium
H.U.G.S. (GED Preparation Class)
Handicapped Ministry
Handyman Ministry
Hard of Hearing Ministry
Helping Out Ministry
Helping Hands
High School Bible Clubs
High School Discipleship
Homeopeners Ministry (Master's Commission)
Hospital Visitation
Human Video Ministry
Hurting Parents Ministry
Husbands' Bible Study
Illustrated Sermons
In Touch & Job Board
Information Rack Ministry
Inner City Camp (I.C.C.)
Intercessory Prayer
InterNet Ministry
Jewish Ministry
Journalism Volunteers Ministry
Journey Out Ministry
Joy Puppets Ministry
Jr. High Discipleship
Junior Deacons
Junior Bible Quiz
Kitchen
L.A. Connection
Loma Gail Women's Home
M.A.P.S.
M.I.R.A.C.L.E.S.
Married Visitation Ministry
Mary Magdalene Ministries
Master's Commission
Medical Lending Closet
Men for Jesus
Men's Life Bible Study
Men's Prayer Meeting
Mill Avenue Outreach
Mission Church Builder
Missionaries (WM's)
Missionary Sponsors (WM's)
Missionettes
Missions (Foreign)
Missions — Mexico
Moms on the Move
Moms
MW's — Senior Men's Ministry
National Street Ministry
Native American Ministry
Nurseries (Infant/Toddler)
Nursing Home Ministry
Offering Counters
Orchestra
Overcomers (Christian 12-Step)
PACT
Pastor's School
Pastoral Care
Pointe Man Ministry
Political Action Ministry
Prayer Chain (WM's)
Prayer Bunch (WM's)
Premarital Encounter Enrichment Program

Appendix 1

Print Shop
Prison Ministry
Prisoners of Hope
Promise Keepers
Publications
R.Y.I.
Refiners Institute
Repairers of the Breach
Revolution
Rodeo
Rose Again
Royal Rangers
Samaritan House (Used Clothing)
Saturday Morning Evangelism
Saturday Morning Soul-winning Society
Security and Traffic Control
Security — Night time
Senior Deacon & Home Visitation
Senior Discipleship Bible Study
Senior Adult Ministry (Trip Co-ordinator)
Senior Fire Institute
Service Set-up Ministry
Set Free Ministry
Shiloh
Shiloh Prayer
Sign Language Interpreting
Single Parents Ministry
Son-Beams (Adult Mentally Retarded)
Soul-winning Mail Out
Spanish Ministry
Special Kids Ministry
Special Dinners (WM's)
Special Forces (Master's Commission)
Speed The Light
Spiritual Gifting Ministry
Standing Firm
Street Evangelism
Sunday Night Live
Sunday School Guides & Greeters (Children's)
Sunday School Guides & Greeters (Adults)
Super Stars Program
Teen Night
Teen Bible Quiz
The Master's Garden
Together Forever Marriage Seminars
TOTS (Sidewalk Sunday School)
Truth Ministry
Ushers — Early service
Ushers
Video
Volunteer Pastors
Volunteers Ministry (Day Care)
Weddings (WM's)
Wheelchair Ministry
Widows Ministry
Wives Prayer Meeting
Wives'Bible Study
Women's Ministry
Women-to-Women Evening Bible Study
XPlosion Outreach
Young Marrieds' Ministry
Youth Choir
Youth Fellowship Families
Youth Missions
Youth Drama

Appendix 2:
Ministries at Los Angeles International Church

Adopt-A-Block Ministry
After Service Feeding Homeless Ministry
AltemaUve Music Ministry
Asphalt Ministry
Audio Tape Ministry
Audio Team
Basketball League
Boxing/Karate Ministry
Breakers For Christ
Buisnessman's Ministry
Bus Ministry
Bus Maintenance Ministry
Cambodian Children's Choir
Cambodian Ministry
Carnalas Lo-rider Bike Ministry
Christian Counseling
Church on the Beach
Classic Car Ministry
Clothing Ministry
Clown Ministry
Community Cleanup Program
Cooking Ministry
Creative Decorations Ministry
D.C. Productions
Detox Ranch
Discipleship Program
Dog Ministry
Drama Workshop
Dream Center
Filipino Church
Filipino Visitation
Fishing Ministry
Free Community Gift Shop
Fundraising Ministry
Gangstaz for Christ Ministry
Gay Ministry
Ghetto Cruiser
Golfers for Christ
Graffiti Cleanup
Healing Ministry
Hip Hop Ministry
His Hand Extended
Hispanic Ministry
Home School and Tutoring Ministry
Hope For Hollywoods' Homeless
Hospital Visitation Ministry
Human Video
Illustrated Sermons
Incense Ministry
Inner City Soccer League
International Friendship Cruises
International Dreams Christian Car Club
Jesus Christ Productions
Junior Church Ministry
Juvenile and Prison Ministry
King of Kings University
Korean Ministry
LAIC Band
LAIC Book Store
LAIC Chaplain
LAIC Flower Shop
LAIC Praise & Worship Team
LAIC Prayer Tower Ministry
LAIC Singers
LAIC Youth Ministry
Ladies' Fellowship
Letter Writing Ministry

Appendix 2

Literary Program
Los Angeles Multi-Purpose Program (L.A.M.P.)
Maps Team
Marriage Ministry
Matt Crouch Video Department
Medical Clinic Ministry
Messianic Fellowship
Metro Kidz
Mission Hotel
Music/Vocal Arrangement, Composition, Production, & Performance
National Filipino Ministry
New Member Visitation
Newcomers' Ministry
Our Daily Bread
Outreach Coordinator
Overcomers' Ministry
Overseas Ministry
Pastor Phil's Biker Church
Phone Bank Ministry
Photography Ministry
Plumbing Ministry
Prayer And Healing Ministry
Reach for the Stars Ministry
Roller Hockey Ministry
Russian Ministry
Russian Bus Ministry
Sailors For Christ
Servants For Christ Motorcycle Ministry
Set Free University Studies
Set Free Posse
Short Term Youth Mission
Skid-Row Ministry
Songbird Productions
Sound Team Ministry
Spanish Ministry
Surfers For Christ
T-Shirt Ministry
Teen Talk
TV Production Studio
Under the Influence (Band)
Unwed Mothers Ministry
Voice & Piano Coaching Ministry
West Coast Flava
Wheelchair Ministry
Wheelchair Basketball League
Wheelchair Hockey League
Young Warriors
Youth Basketball League
Youth Bible Study

Enlarge Your Circle of Love!

For more information about the Los Angeles International Church and "The Dream Center" housed on the campus of the former Queen of Angels hospital, please call or write:

Los Angeles International Church
P. O. Box 26629
Los Angeles, CA 90026
Phone: 213-207-2750

The Dream Center welcomes inquiries from youth and adult groups wishing to come and do mission work at the church. All prayers, contributions and inquiries about ministry and financial support are welcomed.

For information about upcoming Pastors' and Leaders' Schools, or about the *Soul-Winners Training Course* used to train leaders and workers, call or write:

Phoenix First Assembly
13613 N. Cave Creek Road
Phoenix, AZ 85022-5185
Phone: 602-867-7117

If you enjoyed *Multiplication*, we would like to recommend the following books:

There's a Miracle in Your House!
by Tommy Barnett
God wants to do something fantastic with what you already have! This upbeat, motivating book will revolutionize the way you think about "impossible" situations and "overwhelming" opportunities. When God shows you the miracle in your house, you won't have to look anywhere else.

Breaking Intimidation
John Bevere
Is it hard for you to say no? Do you compromise to avoid conflict? Are your decisions based on pleasing others? If you answered yes to any of these questions, *Breaking Intimidation* is for you. This book exposes intimidation, breaks its fearful grip and teaches you to release God's gifts and establish His dominion in your life.